WHAT THE EXPERTS SAY ABOUT
WHATEVER IT TAKES

"Most Inspiring Business Book of the Year! - WOW! Get ready to devour every single page… If you are truly committed to making changes in your business, relationships, or life and are serious about chasing your dreams, this book is for you. Whether you are in sales/business/marketing/entrepreneurship, or simply want to make personal life changes, this book will motivate you to take action."

Jeb Blount, CEO of Sales Gravy and Author of
Fanatical Prospecting

"In 'Whatever It Takes' Brandon Bornancin shares exactly what to do to be wildly successful in sales, business, and life in general. It's rare to find a motivational book that is also a how-to blueprint AND written by someone who not just walks the talk but sprints full speed. If you follow Brandon's advice, you'll reach bigger goals, more quickly!"

Art Sobczak, Author of *Smart Calling*

"This book is for those who want to get out there, put everything they have into their professional and personal pursuits, and not settle! Brandon shares his entrepreneurial and sales journey with such passion and energy, the ideas practically jump off of the pages. 'Whatever It Takes' isn't just a book title, it's the way he shows up in the world. Any seller, leader, or entrepreneur will grow immensely from Brandon's stories and strategies."

Amy Franko, Author of *The Modern Seller*
and *LinkedIn* Top Sales Voice

"If you want to become a champion in sales, and in life, it requires mastering your Self. 'Whatever It Takes' delivers a practical roadmap to conquer any goal. Brandon shares his life's journey, from nothing to failure, and what it really takes to bounce back from adversity, and win. Flip the script on what you think it takes to succeed and discover how to master every area in your life."

Keith Rosen CEO, Profit Builders, Author,
SALES LEADERSHIP and Coaching Salespeople
Into Sales Champions

WHATEVER IT TAKES

MASTER THE HABITS
TO TRANSFORM YOUR BUSINESS,
RELATIONSHIPS, AND LIFE

BRANDON
BORNANCIN

This book is dedicated to you.

My whole life I have lived way below my potential, and never believed that I could achieve all of my dreams.

After doing *Whatever it Takes*, I have finally unlocked the secrets to success and have documented them all in this book to help you do the same.

Your success is the fuel to my fire, and the inspiration for me to go all-out and stay motivated every day.

If this book helps you increase your success, please write a review on Amazon and email me how it helped you at **brandon@seamlessai.com** or via direct message me on Linkedin.

I will send you a very special gift for helping me help other people just like you.

Now let's make this next year your biggest and best yet!

My Best To Your Success,
Brandon Bornancin

CONTENTS

INTRODUCTION

The ability to do *Whatever It Takes* is the most important factor to maximize your success.

You have to overcome your own limiting beliefs to do it, develop the habits to reach your potential, and master the mindset to keep going no matter the obstacles standing in your way.

As an entrepreneur who has closed over $100M in sales and built two eight-figure companies before the age of 30, (including one of LinkedIn's Top 50 Startups) take it from me when I say, it's not easy.

From becoming the richest kid in college on my first venture to losing it all on my second, I learned the times I drastically failed, held the keys to true success.

One of my best-kept secrets? Use failure as fuel. When you fall, use it as the fire you need to get back up. From there, you must be willing to do *whatever it takes*–despite all the odds–to reach your wildest goals.

If you don't invest in this mentality, you will continue to fail, always fall short of your dreams, or worse, give up for good. Having a do-whatever-it-takes mentality is what separates the average earners from the seven-figure earners. This differentiates the dreamers from the doers.

Too many of us sit on dreams like clouds in the sky, only to fall through them onto hard ground. For people with pie-in-the-sky ideas, they will only dream about eating the pie, because it's too far out of reach. It's when they build a ladder up to the clouds that puts the pie in reach.

In other words, you have to build the foundational beliefs, habits, and mindset you need. You must be willing to do *Whatever It Takes* to build your ladder to success.

Success is not only confined to salespeople either. Even though I live and breathe sales, success is for everyone. No matter who you are or what industry you work in, this book will teach you how to do *Whatever It Takes* to reach the level of success you've only ever dreamed about.

WHY I WROTE THIS BOOK

In March 2020, the country shut down due to the COVID-19 pandemic including our office at Seamless.AI (where I am currently the founder and CEO). Even though businesses everywhere were closing their doors and laying off employees, I was determined to embrace the pain and execute the possibilities in what seemed like impossible times.

After making $12M in sales with my first company, but losing it all with my second company (during the worst financial crisis of all time, 2007-2008), I felt more prepared to handle hard times and compelled to write this book.

I originally envisioned writing it as the foundation of my 15-book series called "The Seven Figure Sales System," to help sales teams globally sell any product in any market by developing a bulletproof mentality. However, when COVID-19 hit in March, I felt a sense of urgency to share it with the entire world so they too can learn in uncertain times.

It started when the gyms shut down. Since I had to do my workout routine at home, it meant I had more time to write. In 22 days, I documented the mentality that shaped my upbringing, building two multimillion-dollar companies from the time I was 18, and all the beliefs and habits I have to thank for my success along the way.

Since writing it, my team at Seamless.AI has practiced everything in this book to grow the company over 300%–ALL DURING THE 2020 PANDEMIC! These habits, paired with our Seamless. AI list-building automation technology, allowed us to have zero layoffs and zero salary cuts. We were also fortunate enough to give out nearly 50 promotions!

So instead of keeping this playbook a secret, I decided to share it with you as a way to turn the corner on the past and make this year your best yet. I hope that everything I've documented in this book will help you do just that but achieve it faster and even more successfully than I ever could.

Better yet, this book will work for **anyone**–no matter who you are or what background you come from. We've worked with tens of thousands of companies across every industry and the foundations of this book have proven to be successful time and time again.

THE GOAL OF THIS BOOK

The goal of this book is to help you reach any dream against all odds. Whether you want to transform a relationship, scale your team, start or grow your business, or be more productive in your personal life, my goal is to help you identify your habits that don't work and replace them with empowering ones. Between the battle of your own mind and the pressure of other people, *Whatever It Takes* will teach you how to silence the voice of doubt and fear in your head and replace it with practical habits, mindsets, and beliefs you need to overcome and power through.

In this book, you will learn to identify the limiting beliefs standing in your way to success and what it takes to get rid of them for good. But get ready–this book is not for the faint of heart. This no-b.s. guide will challenge you to admit what's not working about your business or your life and give you the tactics you need to make a positive change.

There will be people who read this book who know their weaknesses but need the motivation to cross the seven-figure threshold. There will also be people who read this who are identifying their weaknesses for the first time ever–giving up their old ways and committing to a new path. Either way, I hope you are one of the people determined enough to do *Whatever It Takes* and apply this book to your life every single day. As you grow, I look forward to hearing about your success. Email me your transformation stories at brandon@seamlessai.com!

HOW TO USE THIS BOOK

The best way to use this book is to read it all the way through, marking certain habits that stand out, or that you want to work on in your life. Also consider reading it with mentors, friends, or accountability partners to help you uncover other areas in your life that could use improvement.

I can't stress the importance of reading this with someone who knows you, works closely with you, and gives you constructive feedback. I recently found an accountability partner on LinkedIn who reaches out to me every single day and pushes me to hit my daily goals. I recommend picking an accountability partner to read this with who will relentlessly challenge you to do *Whatever It Takes.*

I also recommend reading this book multiple times. Keep in mind what you are struggling with today won't go away overnight. It takes repetition to burn new principles into your brain and for them to become natural practices in everyday life.

Also keep in mind the things you struggle with today won't be the same as tomorrow, next week, next month, or even next year. Every time I pick up this book, I am inspired in a new way, so it's the challenge that keeps on giving.

Next time you think you've got it all figured out, go back and read it all again. There's always a new way you can level up in life.

There's always a new way you can level up in life.

1

From Rags to Riches

Don't ever let someone tell you, you can't do something. Not even me. You got a dream, you got to protect it. People can't do something themselves, they want to tell you you can't do it. You want something, go get it. Period.

Will Smith, Pursuit of Happyness

For those of you who don't know me, I'm Brandon Bornancin, just a kid from Cleveland, Ohio.

My parents had no formal college education and worked four full-time jobs just to make ends meet.

My mother worked at a bank during the week and a grocery store at night and on the weekends. During the week, my father sold computer hardware at the May Company (known as Macy's today) and spent nights and weekends working in construction.

I remember when I was growing up how much my family didn't have and couldn't afford. Most of our meals came out of a can and I remember getting teased for wearing oversized T-shirts and ragged shoes. It was a tough experience and I remember it all like it was yesterday.

My mother always lived in scarcity and fear, while my father always dreamed big and aimed to do and achieve more. Ever since I can remember, he had a natural-born, 'whatever it takes' work ethic. However, his ultimate love was selling computers and he knew this type of technology would change the world for the better.

While selling computers at the May Company, he finally got his lucky break.

During one of his shifts, my father impressed a gentleman so much that he not only purchased the most expensive computer, but he also offered my father an interview for a sales analyst role for $22,000 at a high-tech computer startup called Computer Associates (CA Technologies).

Dad couldn't ignore this amazing opportunity to join a tech company building themselves from the ground up. He had a hunch that a new wave of technology was coming and it would revolutionize how people worked and communicated. He thought that if he could get in early, he may have a shot at making some real money and moving up the ranks in a new technology era.

My father started studying and preparing for the interview day and night. When it finally came time, he knew everything there was to know about the company, the products, and how to pitch them.

He was always so insecure about lacking a college degree and thought it would hold him back from ever being considered for the sales role. Luckily for him, this insecurity was a blessing in disguise. It pushed him to wow the interviewer, and then become the hardest-working person in the room.

After getting the job with Computer Associates, my father continued to give everything he had. He traveled to Islandia, New York each Sunday through Friday and was rarely home the first five to eight years of working for the company.

It was difficult for me growing up and wanting to spend as much time with my father as I could. Also a blessing in disguise, it taught me early on to figure things out on my own while my father was doing the same in New York. I knew he didn't want to be away from his wife and kids every week, but he always did whatever it took to provide for our family. I believe this is why I work so hard and give my all, no matter what I do in life.

My father quickly rose to the top of the sales pyramid over the next decade. Every six to 12 months he was promoted and went quickly from sales analyst to account executive, then to sales director, then to the coveted Vice President of Sales role, managing hundreds of top salespeople.

Me enjoying quality time with my father

Throughout his decade-long sales career at CA, he had accomplished massive success building the first B2B software company to ever generate more than $1 billion in sales. Next, he helped work with management to take the company public, which was a massive success!

At the time, my father was one of the highest-paid and widely recognized VPs of Sales in the industry, managing mergers, acquisitions, and thousands of salespeople throughout his career.

Throughout my father's career, our lives changed from rags to riches, all because of sales. Every few years, we moved into a bigger home, bought new luxury cars, wore the best clothes, went to dinner at the nicest restaurants, and went on the most exotic vacations. By the time I was halfway through high school, we lived in one of the largest mansions in our city and I had everything I could ever dream of.

To this day, I can remember when my father took me to one of his big President's Club events in Hawaii. Throughout his 30-plus sales career, he rarely ever missed President's Club.

The room was filled with hundreds of the best salespeople in the world. The awards gala was like a night out at the Oscars or Grammy Awards. Everyone was drinking champagne, eating shrimp, steak, lobster, and all the other delicacies. I was mesmerized.

I remember sitting there, staring at the sea of uber-successful salespeople. My father tapped me on the shoulder and told me: "Hey Brandon, look at all these people here all making over six and seven figures in sales."

"Really?" I asked, in shock.

"Yep," he said.

"Look at John. He made over $1.4 million this year."

"Look at Sarah, she made over $550,000."

"Jeff made over $340,000."

Hundreds of salespeople at the event were all making $100,000, $250,000, $500,000, and many even making more than $1 million in sales.

I was completely blown away.

Then, I had my first big lightbulb moment. All of my counselors and teachers had been telling me that if I wanted to make a lot of money, I had to become an accountant, a lawyer, or a doctor.

Yet, here I was at President's Club with hundreds of salespeople all making over six and seven figures in sales. If you can become a top-producing salesperson, you can become limitless and your earning potential can become limitless too.

Right at that moment, I knew I had to get into sales no matter what it took.

Success in sales is not dependent on a person's pedigree, education, background, or size of their network. Anyone could make it, as long as you put in the work. Sales is the ultimate equalizer. It's the only profession you can make the impossible possible every day.

Every year my father sold for CA Technologies, he won President's Club and I remember asking him how he did it. He always told me it was because of two things:

Build your sales list.

Sell all day and night to the list.

In the early mornings and evenings, he spent all his time building prospecting lists of everyone he needed to sell to. Then during business hours, it was time to sell non-stop to the list.

I witnessed first hand the importance of working hard and learning how to sell. After high school, I attended Ohio University because it was ranked as one of the only colleges with a sales curriculum and one of the top sales schools in the nation. When I was accepted to Ohio University, I knew I had to do two things.

First, I knew I had to find a product that I wanted to sell. My father always told me to be successful in sales, you need to find a product that you would love to sell.

Second, I knew I had to join The Sales Center at OU where I would participate in college-level sales courses, a sales training program, role-playing weekly, and required sales internships.

The first month, I spent all of my time figuring out what the heck I should start selling.

As a big poker player, I recognized the wave of online poker was hitting the country by storm. It was everywhere on TV and college campuses. I couldn't go anywhere without a computer opened with online poker on the screen, or my buddies and I talking about how much we had made or lost.

That was when the second big epiphany hit me.

I asked myself, "What if I just start selling for these online poker companies?"

So I built a list of the poker companies and started cold calling them. After a month of trying to prospect and break in, I finally had a meeting with PartyPoker, FullTilt Poker, and PokerStars.

I pitched all three companies that I could help recruit college students to join their sites. My pitch was centered around that on average, online poker companies earn $1,567 per player. I signed contracts based on them paying me $100 a player!

Boom! Now I had a product I loved and could sell to everyone in my network.

Next, I had to start generating sales.

I started knocking on doors from dorm room to dorm room and had a massive number of students signed up one by one. Boom, one and done.

After signing up nearly everyone in my own dorm room, I went onto the next dorm and signed everyone up. Then I went onto the next building, and the next and the next. I was generating nearly $100,000 in sales and I knew it could easily scale to millions.

I started researching how to build web crawlers and scrapers. After meeting with different engineers on campus, I built my own scraper that would cover all the OU college dorm portals that had a list of all the college students' names and emails. Then, I registered for an email marketing newsletter platform and prepared a mass blast email to everyone.

As a result, I signed up nearly the entire college campus with an interest in playing online poker. After I maxed-out market share at Ohio University, I expanded to other universities nationally. We were starting to do more than seven figures in sales but to scale, I needed to get a website up and we had hit every college campus already. Soon, we were acquiring hundreds of customers per day, all across the nation.

The next three years in college were the best years of my life. My poker marketing company generated $1 million in sales during my freshman year in college, $3 million in sales during my sophomore year, and $6 million in sales my junior year.

Even after a lot of advertising and server costs, I can easily say I was one of the richest kids in college.

From the two-door black Mercedes hardtop convertible, four-door silver Mercedes, GSXR motorcycle, vacation house in Florida, paid-off college loans–I had everything I could ever dream of because I found a product I loved to sell, built a list, and did whatever it took to sell to that list 24/7.

Unfortunately, by the end of my junior year, the online poker industry started to take a downturn and I knew the opportunity wouldn't last. It was time to quit online poker and launch another business. In 2007 and 2008, I took a gamble and bet big on text message marketing on flip phones.

My partners and I took every single penny we made from our first venture and invested it in building a mobile marketing software company called EnMobile.

We secured office space, hired 30 employees, and were on the clock day in and day out. We didn't know anything about building software, B2B sales, or how many millions we would need to develop a scalable product that could support Fortune 500 customers.

We worked our asses off for the next three years, every single day, but the venture was an epic failure. We couldn't generate sales because we didn't know how to find the B2B sales lists to sell to. Over the course of those next three years, we lost everything we had ever made from the prior poker-marketing venture. Eventually, we had to turn the lights off and shut it all down.

By this time, I had graduated from college and was completely broke. I had gone from being the richest kid on campus to bankrupt with a negative checking account balance. Sure, I was still driving my two-door Mercedes hardtop convertible but I couldn't afford to pay for the gas to drive the damn thing.

After a brutal second entrepreneurial business venture, I knew I was ready to call it quits on entrepreneurship and go back to my roots in sales.

My business partners from EnMobile pitched me to join them and start selling seven and eight-figure websites and custom software products to other marketers and IT people at IBM.

Over the next few years, I sold multimillion-dollar deals for IBM and then eventually left to sell for Google and their top search marketing agency.

Throughout my career at IBM and Google, we generated a few million dollars in sales but we always struggled to be ultra-successful. Plain and simple, we were wasting all of our time in sales on endless manual list building, endless manual prospecting, endless manual CRM data entry, and endless manual appointment setting work.

I knew that my father won the President's Club every year because he had the sales lists and always sold 24/7 to those lists. My first company did the same. My second company was a complete and utter failure because we didn't.

So I pitched management at IBM and Google to get the budget of $500,000 to $1 million to invest in sales lists from three different databases.

When we interviewed all these sales database providers, they all told us, "Yeah, we've got all those people in our database.

You just have to give us $300,000, $500,000, $100,000, etc. " depending on the provider. Eager to get started, we agreed and wrote the big check to access their databases.

The first time we ever logged in, we were dumbfounded. The databases only had a few thousand people that matched the title and company criteria that we needed. In reality, there were more than 500,000 ideal decision-makers and prospective customers online.

We were missing more than 90 percent of the people we needed. When they did have 10 out of the 10,000 people we needed, nearly 75 percent of them had the wrong emails, wrong phone numbers, no cell phone numbers, or were no longer working at the same company. Even worse, many were deceased.

I was furious. My team was furious. And we were concerned about losing our jobs.

I could have freaked out, quit, and started job searching because I knew I would get fired after I just pitched management that this massive investment would solve all of our sales goals and dreams. Instead, I called all of my engineering friends at IBM, Google, and other networks. I pitched them that we had to get together to brainstorm and build something that is going to revolutionize the sales space. I remember setting the stage at the meeting by asking my friends: "How do we fix this problem?"

It was then I had my third biggest life epiphany and this one was revolutionary.

"What if IBM & Google were combined for sales?"

"Google built a search engine to find any information across the web in one search," I explained to the group.

"What if *we* built a search engine like Google did, but our own search engine aims to find people with the current titles working at the current companies instantly? That way we find the most updated information for everyone we need to sell to in one click?"

"We could build our own real-time, people search engine!"

I knew once we had that list and could pull off actually building our own search engine, we could create our own AI technology. If IBM Watson could use artificial intelligence to research anything in real-time, we could build our own 10-step AI engine to research, validate and verify a B2B contact's perfect email and phone numbers across billions of data points.

The rest was history.

Everyone who brainstormed with me that day loved the idea. We took it and ran with it.

From there, we started building a search engine powered by artificial intelligence that delivered the world's best sales leads. It would eventually be used by over 100,000 sales teams, marketers, and entrepreneurs to maximize sales.

Later, we would call our search engine Seamless.AI and we would use it to research, validate, and verify perfect emails and phone numbers for anyone in the world *in real-time.*

We used our prototype to generate more than $100 million in sales while selling for IBM and Google. That's when it hit me like a ton of bricks:

THE BIGGEST "AHA" EPIPHANY MOMENT OF MY LIFE.

I remember like it was yesterday. While in my second year selling for Google, I landed in Vegas for a big poker conference. It was a Friday morning, at 9 a.m. Vegas time, when my accountant woke me up.

"We've got a problem," she said. "If I pay you $137,000 in one month in sales commissions, taxes are going to just destroy your commission payout. How do you want this sliced up?"

"What do you mean, 'How do you want this sliced up'"? I queried.

"You meant to say a $13,000 commission check, right?" I asked, baffled.

"No," she said. "Brandon, you were in so many back-to-back pitches and closed so many deals that we owe you $137,000 for this month's sales commissions and that's before your salary."

At that moment, I sat back and stared at the Cosmopolitan hotel room ceiling, speechless.

My buddy Steve in the bed to the right of me looked at me saying "Are you ok, bro?"

"Holy shit, I just made over six figures in sales commissions in just one month," I thought, in shock.

Right then and there, I knew if I could do it using the power of Seamless and our *Seven-Figure Sales System*, anyone in the world could do it too and I have to be the person to help them get there ASAP.

Instead of selling for IBM and Google making *them* millions and billions in sales, I had to help every salesperson, marketer, and entrepreneur in the world generate millions in sales with Seamless.AI, and I set out to do exactly that.

We had no choice but to take all the money we ever made using Seamless to go all-in on investing every penny into building Seamless from the ground up so others can accomplish the same.

From that moment on, I knew I had to do *Whatever it Takes* to go all-in on this one thing and develop the habits, mindset, and belief systems that would allow me to overcome any obstacle that presented itself. It was in fine-tuning my mental attitude, I was able to reach more success (not just for me, but for others) than I ever imagined possible. It was in doing *Whatever it Takes* in all capacities of my own life that led me to write this very book for you today.

2

Get Ready to Do Whatever it Takes

You need to go from just surviving, to thriving, because your life, family, and legacy depend on it.

If you are anything like me when I started out in sales, marketing, and entrepreneurship, you struggled to find success. Finding the reason to stay zeroed on your goal and remind yourself every day why you're doing all this hard work will help you go all out, do whatever it takes, and never make excuses.

Maybe you want to make more money to build the life you always wanted for your family.

Maybe you want extravagant vacations, or to live in a big mansion or drive fancy luxury cars.

Maybe you just want to make enough money to pay for the bills and put food on the table, but you have absolutely no idea what to do or how to get started.

Maybe, like me, you see all the gurus on TV commercials, Instagram ads, and Facebook pictures all making a ton of money, driving Lamborghinis. They say they are "only working four hours a week" because they have created a passive income automation machine where you get rich barely doing anything.

Maybe you want to get into sales to make unlimited earning potential and not be a prisoner to the hourly rate requirement. Yet, no matter how hard you try to sell, you can't overcome the "how."

Maybe you have been trying to generate seven figures in sales, have failed countless times, and wonder if it's just you who can't be successful and only you who is destined for failure.

Maybe you know you must be doing something wrong, but you can't figure out what it is.

If this is you or has been you, I can promise you, I have been in your shoes. I've struggled before to grow my business, generate sales, increase my revenue, and maximize my income.

I've struggled with generating seven figures in sales. I've read every sales book I could get my hands on to get all the advice I could get from the "sales gurus" and "geniuses." Then, I just sat back with hundreds of pages of written notes while feeling completely lost, dazed, and confused.

I've bought all these programs searching for the "limitless" magic pill to cure all my sales pain and bring in the qualified appointments and sales on 100 percent auto-pilot.

Out of all the books, courses, experts, and training from people who looked like they "had it all," it's hard to follow which ones really worked.

Oftentimes, I found they even contradicted each other. One book would recommend that I go follow Plan X when in reality, it was the exact opposite of what would have really moved the needle to maximize sales for my particular business.

Relying on these so-called experts felt like I was jumping on a new fad diet and, after weeks of trying it, gaining more weight than I had before. I was chasing this "new fad," "new technology" or "new idea." Each "new shiny object" distracted my focus from one thing to the next, which only led to constantly generating the same or fewer results.

All of this hard work studying, reading, buying, exploring, testing, researching, and listening to different recommendations never produced seven figures in sales. It actually took my focus away from what I should have really been doing — going all-in on what worked for me.

I kept doing this until I discovered the system that all of the top performers, millionaires, and experts were using to generate millions in sales and maximize their fortunes.

What I reveal in this book is the proven, battle-tested habits, beliefs, and mindset attributes that all the top performers and I use to make more than seven figures while maximizing our company's success today.

Read through this list and mentally note which of these thoughts has run through your head:

Before, I always wanted to generate $1 million in sales but never believed it was possible.

I never believed I was smart enough.

I could never stay motivated.

I had no sales network.

I was not a natural-born salesperson.

I didn't want to sound slimy and sleazy.

I felt like I was selling my soul to do it.

I continued to waste time with prospects that went nowhere.

I never knew how to respond and overcome objections to close the sale.

Cold calling, emailing, social selling simply was not working.

No matter what I did, I couldn't book the appointments on my calendar needed to close more sales.

My prospects were never responding to my outreach.

I could never create sales campaigns that stood out or helped my businesses attract a consistent flow of clients.

I could never get any referrals from my network.

I never had enough sales experience.

I could never get the funding I needed.

I could never succeed no matter how hard I worked.

After trying every outbound sales strategy under the sun, I have had little to no luck at all.

No matter what sales book or expensive training I paid for to teach me the way, most of the information out there was terrible and didn't fit my personality or communication type.

After trying every sales strategy under the sun, I could never get close.

Do any of these things sound like you? The good news is, you have the power to move beyond these perceived barriers and into a life where your hard work pays off with a lot less frustration.

After A LOT of experimenting over 15 years, I eventually found the things that worked. (Most of which were counter-intuitive and the exact opposite of all the advice that all the gurus and supposed sales experts were telling me!).

With a lot of trial and error, I figured out the key to overcoming all these limiting beliefs. Now, I teach my system to salespeople everywhere who face the same list of doubts, so they can generate a steady flow of meetings with their ideal clients.

You can too!

Though I want to preface by saying, what I am about to share is *not* for the faint of heart. This book is *not* for someone who doesn't want to improve their mindset in business, relationships, or life. Even if you want that, this book is *not* for someone who isn't willing to do *Whatever it Takes* to commit to making big changes to achieve it. If you want it, you have to give it everything you've got.

In this book, I break down how you can overcome the most overlooked key to success–the obstacles of your mind and how to execute the possibilities.

If you are serious about doing *Whatever it Takes* to maximize your health, wealth, and potential, then I am serious about helping you achieve it. You get out of this exactly what you put in. Let's make that commitment together, right now, to make reading this book the most intense, eye-opening experience of your life.

TO MAKE YOUR COMMITMENT, SIGN YOUR NAME HERE:

_____

Now, say it with me out loud: "I CAN DO ANYTHING."

Let's dive in.

3

Break Bullsh*t Beliefs

*The top one percent of performers do not let other people's opinions and beliefs hold them back from living the life they want. **Your habits, mindset, beliefs,** and choices can be changed at any time — no matter who you are, where you are going, what you believe, or what you are going through.*

To do this, you need to aggressively eliminate all of the self-doubts and limiting beliefs holding you back from maximizing your success. We all have them and they sound like:

"I can't do this."
"I don't deserve that."
"I will never be successful."
"I suck at this."
"I am a phony and no one will believe me."
"I don't have the intelligence, work ethic, productivity, background, location, or network to be successful."

You have to ban these thoughts. Tell them to f*ck off and never listen to them again. You deserve to be successful and you have what it takes to be successful. You are amazing, you are smart and you are powerful.

If you believe that you will fail, most likely you will fail. You can decide to do either one and both require the same amount of work. You need to recognize what the mind can believe, the mind can achieve. This is why it's critical to develop positive can-do habits and mindset beliefs.

Success in life is based on about 10 percent of what happens to you and 90 percent how you respond, believe, and react. So let's confront some of those habits that are holding you back and replace them with a kick*ss mental attitude to get your butt in full gear.

Choose to substitute your destructive habits, mindsets, and beliefs with ones that will promote growth along your journey to seven-figure success.

Make the choice today, to do *"Whatever it Takes"* to go all out for yourself and prepare to win big. Before we dive in, it's important to prepare. After all, I believe luck is what happens when preparation and opportunity meet. If you are prepared, something good is bound to come along. Here's an example that might help you mentally prepare for the contents of this book, just as it prepared me for the life I'm living now:

DEVELOP CONSTRUCTIVE PARANOIA

My father raised my sister and me with extreme "constructive paranoia." While he became a top salesperson in the president's club, he always remembered coming from a poor family and what it took to make more money than he could have ever dreamed of.

Extreme constructive paranoia helped us believe that everything could be taken from us at any given time. No matter what we were doing, or who we were with, it was critical to stay humble, hungry and the hardest workers in the room every single day.

So while you are producing great sales results and things are going well, you still need to remain hyper-vigilant and cautious.

Assume that sales or market conditions will turn against you at the worst possible times and always plan and prepare accordingly.

Ultimately, I hope this book will help you to build a foundation for success, stay grounded, and always work as hard as possible despite any success you attain. Be on high alert and get prepared for battle, because you could lose it all at any moment. That starts with first eliminating all the bullsh*it holding you back and replacing it with new habits, beliefs, and secrets that can help you to rebuild your life and transform your success.

DON'T BUY THE GET-RICH-QUICK SCHEMES

Do you know what's funny? Every get-rich expert out there who sells the "get-rich-quick schemes" works their a$s off. To sell the get-rich-quick idea successfully, they all have to work seven days a week.

It's a grind. To get rich, you have to work your a$s off for seven days a week.

I know the formula, so I'm going to share it with you.

#1. Find a great product to sell.

#2. Get a sales list of people to sell to.

#3. Sell 18 hours a day, seven days a week, and work your a$s off.

Doing these three things comes with sacrifices. You'll have to give up seeing your friends and family, give up downtime, give up hobbies, give up everything to focus on these things. Then, you will get filthy rich.

Oh and by the way, consider the probability that you will have to maintain that focus for 10 years straight to reach ultimate success.

Those who do it, don't hang out with friends and don't do anything at all but work from 6 a.m. until 10 p.m. every single day.

That's the reality of it.

I can testify.

"Getting rich quick" is a ridiculous idea. That's why they call it the "get-rich-quick-scheme". It's a *scheme*, and it simply does not exist in reality.

If you want to get rich quick, you have to put in the work. The end.

ELIMINATE YOUR BULLSH*T EXCUSES

Stop coming up with reasons why you can't get to The Seven Figure Club.

We all want to avoid putting in the hard work and sacrifices to get to where we want to go, mainly because we aren't 100 percent sold on doing whatever it takes to get there… When we aren't all-in on transforming ourselves, we make up excuses like:

- *"I don't have time."*
- *"I don't have an education."*
- *"Now is not a good time."*
- *"It's too expensive."*
- *"I'm too busy."*
- *"It's too hard.*
- *"It's too early."*
- *"It's too cold."*
- *"It's too hot."*
- *"This sales channel doesn't work."*
- *"My product sucks."*
- *"My company isn't very good."*
- *"My manager is bad."*

I could do this all day. We could come up with 100 different reasons why we won't be successful. Right now, you need to eliminate all those bullsh*t excuses that tell you why you can't accomplish something.

Excuses have killed more sales goals and dreams than anything out there. Don't let them hold you back from creating the life, family, marriage, and future you want.

"Excuses are dream killers. If we allow them, our excuses will keep us locked in a prison of our own making. As the adage goes, if you argue for your limitations, you get to keep them."

– Marie Forleo

If you tell me, "The timing isn't right," I'll tell you, the timing is never right! Do you know what the best time is to do something you always dreamed of doing? Right now! Not later. It will never happen later.

"It's not a good time," is just a limiting belief. Eradicate it and move forward.

Accept that you will never have extra time. It's always better to get something done versus waiting for the perfect time to do something or avoid completing a project or task until you feel that it is perfect. Get great at getting things done and moving onto the next set of tasks vs. waiting forever to achieve perfection.

STOP B*TCHING ABOUT THE PAST AND GO CREATE THE FUTURE

Many of the people I know, from friends and family members to people in my network, constantly complain about how they grew up. They allow their past to create resentment within them then use it as an excuse for not reaching their goals. Stop complaining and b*tching about the past. It's the past.

You need to get over it, then go create the future with everything you learned from the past. I could complain all day and night about my childhood or bad things that happened to me.

No one cares.

For example, I barely saw my father growing up. It affected me quite a bit because my mother came from an abusive background and was nowhere near stable enough to raise two kids. Every Sunday, my dad would fly to New York then back Friday evening. I only had two days with him while he was grinding on the road the other five.

My mom worked two full-time jobs to pay the bills and the childcare facility. I remember crying and fighting with my mom about having to go to the sketchy daycare and never getting to see my father. I just didn't think it was fair. Yet, my mom continued supporting my father, explaining he was gone so he could provide for the family.

However, those years taught me to never to be coddled. They taught me to do whatever it takes to provide. I learned that no matter what I want in life, I have to go out and work hard to go get it, regardless of any past events that tripped me up.

The moral of the story is, stop using your past as a blocker to create an amazing future for you and your family. Bad things happen to all of us but you can learn from them to build a better tomorrow.

MAKE MORE MONEY; DON'T SAVE MORE MONEY

Stop living with a scarcity mindset. You should be trying to expand, not retreat. Every time I talk about this habit, I remember the way my parents acted during my childhood.

My mother, unfortunately, was emotionally abused as a child. As a result, she was always anxious about losing our home and having to live on the streets. She would spend all weekend cutting coupons and going to garage sales to save as much money as possible.

My mom would also hoard products in the house because she thought Doomsday would happen any second. I remember one time there was a coupon rebate for toothpaste where the toothpaste was 50 percent off and if you mailed in the rebate, you actually made $1. My mom and uncle bought 100 bottles of toothpaste.

As a kid, I was thinking, "What the f*ck do you need that much toothpaste for?" They were in a constant crisis mode, saving money because they were scared the world was going to end.

Now, my father, on the other hand, was the complete opposite. Even though he came from a poor family and didn't have much money growing up, he had a growth mindset.

I remember he would tell me stories about him and his three brothers kicking rocks in the driveway and playing with sticks because they had nothing else to play with.

That being said, he always wanted to work hard and make more money. Once he started to, he would pay people to do the things that cost less than what he would make per hour. He recognized the value of making money, not saving it.

Throughout his journey from sales in a tech startup to the first billion-dollar software company, my father would spend all day and night focused on making money and selling. If he had to do anything that didn't correlate to generating more sales for his company, he outsourced it. Eventually, we started to get wealthy and he would pay cleaners, lawn people, cooks, etc.

You can only save so much money with what you make. However, your earning potential is limitless.

Don't save money. Focus on investing in ways to make more money.

ACCEPT THAT YOU ARE ENTITLED TO NOTHING IN THIS LIFE

If you think everything is going to go your way because you are smart, beautiful, talented, and living in the right country, you will be in trouble when things don't go as planned and life smacks you in the face.

Living life like you are entitled to anything is playing with fire. There will always be someone right around the corner who knows that they have to earn every penny they get in this lifetime and they will fly right past you and any other person who is moving slowly or waiting for their handout.

Being entitled is toxic and it can kill your sales goals and dreams. You need to have the right mindset to work hard and the most likely struggle for anything and everything you get in this life. That is far closer to reality than believing you are entitled to anything.

Typically, the people who struggle and fight like hell always beat the people with an entitled mindset— especially in the long run.

Life is not easy. It never will be, so do not try to make it that way.

Life is not fair. It never was, it isn't now, and it will never be.

Don't fall into the trap of entitlement. Don't let yourself believe you are a victim when you are not.

Get over it and get on with it

Life gets a little bit easier and fairer when you put in the work and accept responsibility for everything.

Additionally, most things are more rewarding when you break a sweat to get them.

There is nothing more debilitating in life than a bad attitude. I've met people facing the most difficult situations of loss, handicaps, and disease, who maintain a great attitude and live fulfilled lives. Attitude is everything.

A victim mindset, hatred, prejudice, entitlement, all of these cornerstones of a bad attitude will only hold you back from your success and happiness. You can increase the likelihood of your success just by changing the way you view things in your life.

We will all have things that happen that are good and bad, whether it's life or death, marriage or divorce, successes, or failures. For example, look at the Great Depression, the Great Recession of 2007-2009 which brought the collapse of the housing bubble, the collapse of the dot-com bubble in the early 2000s, or the coronavirus pandemic happening as I write this book. All of these recessions and economic collapses can either make you stronger, smarter, and better, OR they can make you poorer, weaker, and worse.

Your attitude and how you embrace times of adversity will mentally make you or break you. The best part is, you get to decide!

We can be grateful for things that happen and learn from them, both good and bad. Or we can hate the things that happened to us and think the world is against us.

What will you choose?

TREAT REJECTION AS THE DATA NEEDED FOR RATIFICATION

I've had hundreds of venture capitalists pass on investing in Seamless and our vision to positively impact 1 billion people.

The feedback pitching all these venture capitalists was the same:

"Your market is not good enough."
"Your idea is not good enough."
"Your team is not good enough."
"Your education is not good enough."
"Your product is not good enough."
"Your development background is not good enough."
"You're not good enough."

Whatever bullsh*t they had on their little Excel financial projection scorecard told them we "weren't good enough."

I respect them for that though, because they are protecting their investors, which I have grown to appreciate.

That being said, I got rejected by hundreds of investors and VCs.

After hearing, "Brandon, right now it's a pass, but keep up the good work. We'll look at investing in the future," it hurt badly. It was f*cking terrible.

But I would always ask:

"Please tell me why. Please tell me the no-bullsh*t reason why."

Then, I would go write it down and learn from all of their honest feedback. I would go back to the office and continue selling, building, iterating, optimizing, hustling, and developing.

Fast forward to today and we are growing 50 to 100 percent month over month.

Now, we are turning down multimillion-dollar venture capital investment offers.

My advice for all of you out there with a sales dream, marketing dream, entrepreneurship dream, or any life dream, is simple:

NEVER F*CKING QUIT.

Rejection is not the end of a road; it is a sign you need to adjust your strategy.

STOP LIVING FOR THE WEEKENDS

If you never stop living for the weekends, that is all you will ever have.

When I was in high school, the only thing I was excited about was the weekend. I wanted to party all day, hang with my friends, go out to pick up girls, get wasted — you name it.

I had no purpose in life. I had no goal and no vision of the future I wanted.

I realized before going to college that I wanted to go into sales and launch my own company. I found a goal, a mission, and a purpose to start working towards and fighting for.

Instead of living for the weekend, I was living to beat the sun up in the morning and get in as many hours as humanly possible. When I got to Ohio University and launched my online poker marketing company, I couldn't wait to wake up every single day.

I would wake up early at 5 a.m., jump on the poker forums, and direct message people in the old school chat forums for three to four hours, telling them to visit my website. At 8 a.m., I would close the computer and head to PING (our college gym) to get an amazing workout in, then I'd go back to my dorm to start knocking dorm-room to dorm-room to sell people on joining my site.

After knocking on all the doors in a college dorm building, I would then go back to my dorm room to start figuring out who else I could start prospecting and selling. Where else could I build a list of people to sell to? Anywhere I went, any single day, I was selling them to buy my product and the people loved it.

I knew I was helping people play a game they loved to play. I was generating $10 million in sales for all the poker companies I represented and it was amazing.

But none of that happened until I looked around and noticed a few things.

All of my friends at the time were average deadbeats. They had no goals, they had no dreams and they had no massive vision. They just wanted to slog through the week, put in minimal work, and then party all weekend.

I finally started living every day to accomplish my goals and dreams because I knew if I continued to live for the weekend, that's all I'd ever have.

You have to do the same. You have to embrace new habits.

FIND SOLUTIONS, NOT PROBLEMS

Train your mindset to take a step back, research all the options, evaluate the pros and cons, then implement the solution that will maximize your success for the given problem.

In sales and entrepreneurship, you will be faced with thousands of problems, professionally and personally.

- Problems with prospecting.
- Problems with appointment-setting.
- Problems with closing.
- Problems with cold-calling and emailing.
- Problems with social-selling,
- Problems with pitching,
- Problems with negotiating,
- Problems with commissions and the economy.

You will have problems with prospects' businesses shutting down or even thriving.

No matter what we do, in sales and entrepreneurship, we will be faced with thousands of problems and challenges every year.

It's critical to train your brain to be excited about solving these new challenges because every challenge or problem has a solution. I have never encountered a problem for which I couldn't find multiple potential solutions.

For example, I wanted to build a real-time search engine to find people to sell to, then I had a dream to use a 10-step artificial intelligence engine to research, validate and verify perfect, current emails and phone numbers for all my prospects.

Here was this massive idea, yet, I was the least qualified person in the world to figure out how the hell to build it.

I was just some guy from Cleveland who grew up in a poor family and got into sales. Then, I went into sales and entrepreneurship because it was what I knew best.

I didn't study computer science, programming, artificial intelligence, or search engine applications. But guess what I did? I listed out my problem along with all the possible solutions.

Problem: I am sick and tired of being held hostage by outdated sales databases that are missing 90 percent of the contacts you need. When they do have the right people, the emails always bounce back and they never have the correct phone numbers or direct lines.

My first solution to solving this problem was to study and learn how to build search engines and the architecture of search engines. After spending months reading every book on the topic, I drew up the architecture.

I knew I wasn't going to be able to build the search engine on my own so I started to prospect for the people who could help me. For example, I identified the back-end engineers who had experience in search and databases.

We then hired the right engineers, built the Seamless.AI platform, and generated millions in less than a year. Now, we employ more than 100 people (October 2020), help more than 100,000 salespeople, marketers, and entrepreneurs, and are scaling to have 250 employees before the end of the year (all during the Coronavirus pandemic!).

This is all because I trained my brain and mindset to become limitless in my search for solutions to the problems I encounter.

I believe that every problem has a solution. You need to commit to finding all possible solutions, evaluating the pros and cons for each, then testing your decision by executing it using data.

If it doesn't work, that's okay. Try another solution, then another. And another. Until you run out of options to solve the problem. Focus on your progress and keep looking ahead.

The great news is, you will never run out of options. There are always more ways to solve a problem. Don't throw in the towel. Keep searching and recognize that every problem has a solution. You just have to shift your focus from the problem to the solutions.

YOUR PAST DOESN'T DEFINE YOUR FUTURE

When you come from a bad place or experience a traumatic upbringing, a lot of people might write you off.

They think you aren't supposed to make it.

For the majority of my childhood, I grew up in a poor family. But, I use that as motivation to never be poor ever again and to work hard to accomplish my dreams. Just because you grew up differently than someone else doesn't mean that those circumstances define who you are and who you will become.

Don't listen to the naysayers and non-believers. The best part about the past is it's the past. You can forget about it and focus on making your future bright. Accept full responsibility for your own fate and reject the mindset and notion that outside forces will dictate your destiny.

The sales you win will be because of things that you did; the sales you lose will be because of the things you didn't do. You control your successes and your failures, not anyone or anything else.

Say it with me: "If it's meant to be, it's up to me!"

Your success today and going forward is not dependent on the past.

MAKE GOOD CHOICES OR BAD CHOICES. YOU DECIDE

You are a collection of the choices you make.

You need to consistently look at your choices and categorize them as good or bad decisions. The ultimate goal is to only make great decisions that move you towards accomplishing your goals.

For example, I'm not a big drinker but on the weekend, I may have a drink or two so my brain slows down and stops thinking about work. This is what I call a bad decision. I shouldn't need to use alcohol or any substance to "turn off my brain."

I know my sleep, weight loss and productivity will be negatively impacted by this one bad decision the next day. Luckily, I don't do it frequently and often, but when I do, I know this one decision is going to give me short-term satisfaction but not any long-term gain.

Instead, I can meditate, go for a run, do yoga, or just take a few deep breaths. I go on extended stretches of 30 days to 300 days without alcohol to clear my mind and body of any toxins or decreases in productivity (yes, this is an extreme example).

The point is, every day, you are making good choices that move you towards accomplishing your goals, or you are making bad choices that are moving you away from accomplishing your goals.

You get to decide.

Document the good and bad choices you are making every day and try to get rid of the bad while stacking up the good! Over time, you will maximize your success and your potential.

YOU ARE ONLY IN COMPETITION WITH YOURSELF

The only reason anyone criticizes someone else going after their goals and dreams is that they have something deep down inside them that makes them wish they had the motivation, inspiration, hard work, time, money, and capital to do the same. They aren't pursuing their dreams, so they are going to chastise and criticize others who are out of jealousy.

Probably 99 percent of the people who criticized me were significantly less successful than I was. I figured this out after being coached and mentored by millionaires and billionaires.

Everyone has a different plan and a different map. Having my goals written down and having my map to get them does not make me a better or worse person than you. I am just different. My goals are not greater or worse than yours. Your goals are not greater or worse than mine. We can both achieve success. It's not a game of someone has to win and someone has to lose. We can both win.

The top one percent of performers do not let other people's opinions and beliefs hold them back from living the life they want.

Millionaires and billionaires realize this. They know they are only in competition with themselves so they try to become the best that they can be and support others around them to get to where they want to go.

When I finally recognized this habit and implemented it in my life, I stopped chastising others and only focused on criticizing myself to get better. I started supporting others to help them get to where they needed to go, regardless of my opinion on their goals and dreams. Then, I went on to become a millionaire.

This is why I feel bad for people who try to bring me down on my pursuit to positively impact others. I know deep down inside, they must be miserable about something related to quitting their goals and dreams. If they didn't quit on themselves, they would never have the time to waste trying to throw sticks and stones at me as I climb the ladder to success.

Be happy with your journey, help others, and focus on improving yourself every day. Don't worry about the miserable people who aren't happy for you. You are your only competition.

DON'T LET ANYONE TELL YOU WHAT YOU CAN OR CANNOT DO

There will be many times in your career where you need to ignore what the world thinks you can accomplish.

I never let a sales manager determine my sales potential. I never let a venture capitalist tell me if my idea would be a success or not. I never let a teacher or a family member tell me that I could or couldn't do something.

You need to reject what the world thinks that you can accomplish, and just go do it. Set your goals, track your progress, and achieve your seven-figure sales results.

Only you get to determine what you can or can't do.

If you want to accomplish something that you have never accomplished before—or even that no one has accomplished before, then go do it. Research it, develop the action plan, then put in the work.

Don't let anyone ever tell you what you can or cannot do.

COMMIT TO CONSTANTLY GROW AND IMPROVE

Most people think that if they become super-rich and acquire success, wealth, the mansion, the fastest growing startup, the prettiest wife, a spot on the Forbes 30 Under 30 list, it is going to change their life forever and fundamentally change them.

Let me tell you something… it really doesn't.

I am a living, breathing example that while you can be motivated by accomplishment, you can't be motivated by pride. Pride consumes the weak and kills your ability to achieve success.

I know this because I bought the hard-top two-door convertibles in cash when I was 18.

I know this because I bought the Florida vacation house I spent time at during college.

I had the prettiest girlfriends as my companies were thriving.

Although having all the products and recognition made me feel good, it didn't change anything.

None of it really meant sh*t.

When I was 22, I wanted the cars, houses, motorcycles, bank accounts, and luxury vacations just to impress people. I realized that I was living a life of bullsh*t where every day, all I wanted to do was impress people with how smart and rich I was.

Luckily, I quickly realized this was a "fake news" type of life and within a year, I told myself that I would never let myself worry about impressing other people ever again. I would only focus on setting big goals and achieving them for myself. That's when I truly became the happiest I have ever been in my life and I never looked back.

The greatest fulfillment you can get is from the journey of personal growth, challenge, and accomplishments. The road that takes you from where you are at today to where you want to go to maximize your success.

All the money and the products that you buy (which are awesome by the way, I'm not saying don't get them) won't change anything. The meaning of life is in the journey, almost like a hero movie. You start from the bottom, fight and overcome all these bad guys and problems, then you continue to beat them and you become victorious with everything you ever wanted.

Money and fame don't necessarily buy you happiness. Overcoming your biggest challenges, helping others maximize their success, and personally growing every day does.

P.S. By mastering the above, the ironic thing is you will get all the money, riches, and fame. It's the result of an incredible ride. This reward will make you feel great but not as great as helping people and overcoming your challenges along the way.

PERCEPTION IS REALITY, BELIEVE YOU CAN ACHIEVE

Everything in this world was created and sold by someone no smarter than you. If they can do it, so can you. To generate the life you want through sales, you need to believe that you can do it.

If others can do it, so can you. If someone has done it before, so can you.

There is nothing out there that someone has done that you cannot do.

To generate the results you want, you have to control your beliefs, feelings, and thoughts about yourself. The belief that anything can be achieved will change your life forever. When applied to any goal, problem, or situation throughout your professional or personal life, no problem, obstacle or circumstance will ever hold you back because you can change your approach to tackling them anytime you want.

Changing your mindset will make you unstoppable because you will just adapt to trying new solutions until you find the smartest and fastest way to get where you want to go.

Perception is reality. You need to believe you can achieve. Then, you just have to figure out the smartest and fastest way to get there.

Just remember that no one is perfect. Nothing is ever perfect. Stop trying.

We live in a world and a time right now where people expect perfection. You have to create the perfect life, maintain the perfect marriage, build the perfect family, buy the perfect cars and houses, dress to live throughout life perfectly, and always show others that you and your life are just ideal.

I don't know how this became the criteria for living your life.

You are going to do the wrong things. You are going to make mistakes throughout your life — with your family, within your relationships, among your sales and business peers. No matter how hard you work, you will f*ck up.

The great news is that you need to learn from these mistakes then move forward with the understanding of what not to do next time around.

When you are okay with being flawed, it means that you are fixed!

Now, I am not here to try to discourage you or belittle your accomplishments. I applaud you for everything you have accomplished thus far, but I want to shoot it straight. Too many people get caught up in personal flattery and 'attaboys.

The sooner that you become less impressed with your accomplishments or reaching perfection, and focused on the prospective journey in front of you, the sooner you get to become a whole lot better at doing the things you want to achieve.

GO ALL OUT

Set the bar higher than average.

Average is something to run away from. The average is a trap in a hamster wheel that will run you to death and kill your goals and dreams.

Set your goals higher. Aim to be excellent and extraordinary instead. Make big bets on yourself and make big bets on your future.

Never be satisfied with what you have accomplished in the past. You should always keep pushing forward, upwards, and onwards to achieve more— no matter what.

Crave success as badly as you want to breathe. And remember, although your last breath of air was important, it is not nearly as important as your next. But enjoy the process of each breath. You have to learn to enjoy the consistent, persistent pursuit of your potential. You can either make yourself miserable or enjoy the ride to improve, the amount of work is the same.

Now that you have set your mind to going all-in to achieve your goals, it's time to commit to keeping your brain agile and adapting as life throws curveball after curveball at you. You can only stay at the top of your game if you keep practicing.

4

Define Your Destiny

What you think about, dream about, focus on, and work towards will become your life. You can think small and achieve small or you can think big and achieve big.

I have learned throughout life that **the only people who achieve massive success and change this world for the better are the dreamers**. They are the ones who aspire to accomplish the impossible then go out and make it happen.

If you're reading this book, then you are one in a million. Congrats!

People don't believe they can do something because they have limiting beliefs and fears that hold them back. As you discovered in the previous chapter, your beliefs will make or break you.

- Your beliefs become your thoughts.
- Your thoughts become your words.
- Your words become your actions.
- Your actions become your habits.
- Your habits become your values.
- Your values become your destiny.

What you believe you can do today will define your reality in the future.

It all starts with your belief system.

The only person who limits your ability to achieve seven-figure success or anything you want in life is the person staring back at you in the mirror every single day.

I need you to free your mind and your heart to dream big so you can believe that anything is possible. If you dream small and only believe you can do easy, small things, you will have a life of mediocrity and comfortable happiness (if that). There is nothing wrong with this, but seven-figure producers, earners, and achievers don't believe in dreaming or living on a small scale.

What you think about, dream about, focus on, and work towards will become your life. You can think small and achieve small or you can think big and achieve big.

I will always choose big dreams and massive goals that no one believes I can achieve. Then, I will work towards accomplishing them all. I need you to do the same. I've lived my life way too long (for the majority of it) with small goals, dreams, and aspirations because I was worried about what other people would think. What you believe you can achieve will become your reality.

The person who thinks they can and the person who thinks they can't are both right. You have to decide which person you are.

PLAY OFFENSE, NOT DEFENSE

To become wealthy, financially independent, and able to generate seven figures in sales, you need to play the game of offense, not defense.

When I say 'play offense,' I mean you need to be going all out to maximize your sales, marketing, product development, customer success, and branding— you name it.

Play offense by investing in all the technology that helps you automate list building, make more sales calls, send more emails, post more on social media, deliver more value to your prospects, etc.

One of the major attributes of seven-figure success is generating so much activity on offense that you gain an abundance of leads, appointments, opportunities, sales, and relationships. You aren't dependent on one source of revenue from one channel, one customer, one flow of income, or one opportunity. You have a wide portfolio of investments you've made with all of your activity, time, effort, capital, and resources, so you just keep winning and scoring goals. You turn the odds in your favor.

The only time you can really kick the ball into the net, run the football into the endzone to score the winning touchdown, shoot the game-winning shot to win the championship, etc. is if you are playing offense.

When you play defense, you try to stop others from scoring on you and winning in the game of life. You spend all of your time worrying about what the competition is doing and you live life in a state of fear, retreat, and protection. You are so worried about protecting the very few points that you have, that you will never generate the seven-figure success you are really going for.

Whenever I think about playing offense vs. defense, I think of my mom and dad. My mom worked herself to death for more than 80 hours per week just to make an average income. Then, she would put all of her earnings in the bank to protect them.

She was all about defense. How can I find coupons to save a few dollars? How can I get clothes at garage sales or Goodwill? Now I don't blame her, she had a very tough and poor upbringing that did a lot of damage. She was always scared that one day the very little money she did save was going to be gone. That is not how you want to live life and you will never join the seven-figure club that way.

My father was the exact opposite, even before he built the first $1-billion software company. He worked the same number of hours as my mother but he was always playing offense. He would obsess over how he could create multiple flows of sales deals, opportunities, and commissions. He would be working hard on trying to figure out how he could over-deliver at work to get more raises as fast as possible.

He focused on how he could generate more sales to make more commissions with the least amount of time, work, and effort. He planned how he could build a massive pipeline of relationships and opportunities to generate millions in sales and become financially wealthy and free.

I've experienced life playing both offense and defense, and I choose offense every time. I would rather shoot the ball to win the game and miss, then never shoot the ball at all. I would rather risk it all to win big and go all out with my money, time capital, work, effort, and resources then never try at all.

I'd rather buy all the technology to make me uber-successful and miss on maybe 25 percent of my shots than not invest in the technology at all.

I would rather buy all the books, training, courses, and expensive Masterminds to help me get to where I need to go and get there 10 times faster than if I tried on my own.

If I played defense and was cheap with my money and time, I would never get there at all because I wouldn't get the right coaching, advice, scripts, strategies, or secrets. See what I mean?

The magnitude of your success is calculated by the size of your dreams, the strength of your desire, and your ability to handle failure of epic proportions along the way.

Throughout my life, I've realized the majority of my success can be broken down into a simple mathematical equation with these components:

> **D) = Dream**
> **(D2) = Desire**
> **(F) = Rate of Failure**

If you want to achieve massive success, you just need to multiply **(D) x (D2) x (F) = Size of success.**

Let's say you have a dream to make $100 and, on a scale of 1-10 (10 being your greatest desire), you have a 10-magnitude desire and you run into 5 failures along the way.

We would take **(D)** and replace it with your dream to make $100.

We would take **(D2)** and replace it with your desire of 10.

We would take **(F)** and replace it with your 5 failures.

$$\$100 \times 10 \times 5 = 5{,}000$$

This number — in this case 5,000 — is a value you can use when you compare other dreams you have in front of you at the moment. This simple formula will help you consider the value of your time, your energy, and possible payout in one simple equation. It also assesses your level of risk and tenacity (based on how many false starts you will tolerate) as you prioritize where to invest your resources. Give it a try.

SET SMART GOALS IN ALL FACETS OF LIFE

What are SMART goals?

SPECIFIC: Your goal is direct, detailed, and meaningful.

MEASURABLE: Your goal is quantifiable to track your progress to success.

ATTAINABLE: Your goal is realistic and you have the tools or will find the resources to attain it.

RELEVANT: Your goal aligns with your company or personal mission.

TIME-BASED: Your goal has a deadline.

You need to set specific, measurable, attainable, results-based, and time-specific goals in all areas of your life: your sales, your finances, your health, your emotions, and your relationships.

You can't just say I want to lose weight, I want to be healthy, or I want to make more money. You have to set very specific indicators for these core pillars of your life and track them daily.

For example, if you make $100,000 and you want to make more money, set a specific income target. Maybe you want to go from making $100,000 to making more than $250,000. Or maybe you want to go from making $500,000 to $1 million.

These are very specific and measurable goals that you can track daily to see if you are progressing or going backward.

The greatest part about very specific goals is you can define what you need to do to achieve them on an annual basis, quarterly basis, monthly basis, weekly basis, daily basis, and even an hourly basis. You could literally track how much you need to earn per hour to make $100,000 in sales, $250,000 in sales, $500,000 in sales, and $1 million in sales.

So set very specific, actionable, and measurable goals in all areas of your life such as sales, family, health, relationships, and mental and emotional wellness, then track them daily.

WRITE YOUR BIG GOALS DOWN EVERY DAY AND DREAM BIGGER

You always underestimate what you can accomplish. Even right now! I need you to dream so big that everyone around you thinks you are crazy. Do it no matter what anyone thinks about your goals and dreams.

Write down all of your professional, personal, relationship, health, and family goals down that you want to accomplish right now. Don't bullsh*t yourself.

If you want to make $1 million in sales, write it down. If you want to make $1 million in W2 income in one year, write it down. If you want to get to 10 percent body fat and lose 20 pounds, write it down. Write down all of your professional, personal, relationship, health, and family goals right now.

Next, you should write these goals down at least once a day in the morning and also once a day in the evening. This will keep your mindset focused on achieving all of your goals all day.

This is one of the biggest requirements for joining the seven-figure club in sales.

The second one is to multiply your goals and dreams **by 3, 5, or 10.**

You will always underestimate your potential.

You will underestimate what you can accomplish in a decade.

You will underestimate what you can accomplish in a year.

You will underestimate what you can accomplish in a month.

You will underestimate what you can accomplish in a week.

And you will underestimate what you can accomplish in a day.

This is exactly why you need to multiply your goals by 3,5, or 10. When I generated more than $137,000 in sales commissions in one month and more than $1.2 million in one year, I increased my goals by five times.

It will take years to achieve them. It will be harder than you ever thought. It will require more hard work than you ever imagined. You will experience more failures than you ever have in your life. And you will be greatly disappointed while being greatly uncomfortable going after these 3x, 5x, and 10x goals, but at least they are a much greater representation of what you truly can achieve in this lifetime.

Life is about achievement and constant growth. The only way to recognize your full potential, join the seven-figure club and maximize your impact on this world is to dream big, put in the work, and do the daily activity required to make those big dreams a reality.

BREAK DOWN YOUR DAY INTO DOLLARS

Once you've multiplied your goals and dreams to be more aligned with your true potential, divide those goals into the daily activities you have to execute to achieve them.

For example, say I want to make $250,000 in income per year. I would take $250,000 and multiply it by 3x to 10x. Let's say I move the goal to be better aligned with my full potential and the new goal is $1 million. Now, I want to take that $1 million annual goal and divide it by the number of business days in the year which is around 260.

$1,000,000 / 260 = $3,846 per day is what I need to generate

Next, I want to break that down per hour and even per minute.

$3,846 per day / 10 hours a day = $384 an hour.
$384 / 60 minutes = $6.40 a minute

Now you have the exact breakdown by the minute, hour, and daily activity. You just have to go out there and make it happen, which I believe you can do.

Set bigger goals and dreams because you are likely underestimating your full potential.

TRY TO IMPROVE BY AT LEAST
1% EVERY SINGLE DAY

If you can improve by 1% each day, over the course of a year, that would generate 365 percent growth. However, thanks to the power of compounding, one percent of daily growth can actually generate 3,700 percent growth over a year.

Harnessing the power of the 1% Rule, at worst, you're going to create an improvement of 3.65X, but you could potentially create up to 3,700 percent or 37X more. The truth is, you probably can't imagine this right now. It's too big, bold, and intense. Thirty-seven times better than where you are today is a completely different reality than the one you're living in right now.

At thirty-seven times better than today, you are drenched in achievement and fulfillment. People around you keep asking you for the secret because you're thriving, and they feel it every time they're around you. Don't take this lightly. Use it correctly, and you will never be the same.

KEEP IT SIMPLE

Optimize your actions to achieve all your aspirations and outcomes. Aspiration is something you want in the future. An outcome is a measurable result.

For example:

An aspiration: "I want to increase my sales expertise so I can make more money."
An outcome: Increasing sales expertise and making more money.
An action: "I will read 10 pages of this sales book today."

Make everything that you need to accomplish radically simple. Identify your aspirations, your desired outcomes, and the actions required to achieve them. Then, you can intentionally take small steps in the right direction.

If you want to build all the seven-figure success habits, simplicity rules all. If you want to build a seven-figure success habit, start small and simple.

OVER-COMMIT TO GOALS

Apply a laser focus to accomplishing your goal and eliminate everything and anything that distracts you from it. For example, when I started building Seamless.AI, I cut out the friends, family members, and other people in my network who didn't support me on my mission.

I knew it would be a near-impossible goal to accomplish so I just decided to cut out anything and everything that would hold me back. I also stopped going out with friends or anyone during the week so I could spend 16 to 18 hours a day working on building the platform. To do anything relaxing, fun, or non-work-related on the weekends, I had to earn it.

I would wake up at 5 or 6 a.m., work out, then work until 3 to 5 p.m. to really earn my night out. If I didn't accomplish enough or didn't feel like I truly earned it, I would cancel whatever evening plans I had because I didn't deserve them.

That is what over-committing is all about. I remember family members yelling at me during every holiday "Brandon, why are you working so hard? Brandon, why are you still on the laptop? It's Christmas. It's Easter. It's Thanksgiving." This is what over-committing is about.

Over-committing to your goals is about delaying instant gratification, vacations, time-off, and luxuries, etc., then investing all of your time, energy, capital, and headspace into accomplishing some percentage of your goal. This is the game each and every day on your mission to success.

CELEBRATE YOUR WINS, BIG AND SMALL

You should celebrate a small win you accomplish or experience every single day. These small wins create the momentum and clarity required to accomplish the bigger outcomes we are chasing.

They force us to open up our awareness and feed our inner hero instead of our inner critic. They remind us to not judge ourselves and instead appreciate our growth.

Even if they are small or seem insignificant, celebrate a win every day.

When you win big or achieve something great, celebrate those too.

Whether that is a big deal, a big sale, a big investment, a big partnership, a big interview, a big book deal, a big movie deal—you name it.

These are the moments that you work hard for and that define you and you should not take them for granted.

Cherish and celebrate in those moments.

And then, after you rejoice in your milestone achievement, get back to work bright and early the next morning to win more of them.

Too many people celebrate for too long. While you are celebrating over days, weeks, or months, your competition is putting in the work to pass you by and take you out.

QUIT WATCHING THE NEWS AND INSTEAD GO WORK TO MAKE THE NEWS

When I was 21, I recognized that the news added zero value to my personal or professional improvement so I stopped watching it and never looked back. I feel like it's a brain-washing, time-wasting machine made up by the media companies to sell you ideas, stories, and products. It's always negative and is often used as a scare tactic to increase the emotion of fear and to elicit self-defense mechanisms

I recommend you quit watching the news and instead work on accomplishing your goals and dreams. I've made millions and millions from sales and haven't watched the news since college.

Getting rid of any and all negativity from your life is critical and the news is one of the biggest negativity machines out there.

STOP SPENDING ALL YOUR TIME ON SOCIAL MEDIA AND START MAKING SOCIAL MEDIA

Stop wasting time watching what everyone else is doing and start creating a following by making social media and building a following.

This is very similar to my tip about not watching the news but making the news.

The same goes for social media. I rarely check social media to see what people are doing. Instead, I post on social media and use it to maximize my engagement and build incredible relationships with prospects.

It can be a great tool to help you build up your brand. Otherwise, don't get sucked into spending your time on it.

STAY BROKE THEN BOOTSTRAP TO THE MAX

My first company launched during the housing crisis and my second one during a pandemic. In both cases, my family was going through difficult times, facing bankruptcy and fighting my mom's Alzheimer's Disease, so they didn't have any money to offer. The great news is that you don't need a lot of money to get started or to be successful. All you need is to be extremely resourceful and do whatever it takes.

When we first launched Seamless.AI, we had no money so we had to come up with a commission-based performance-driven sales model. We would pitch 15 demos a day, each of my VP of sales and I, using this commission-based model of prospecting and booking appointments all day.

We went from zero to millions of sales in fewer than 11 months. That would have never happened if we weren't poor, broke, and hungry. When you have a ton of money lying around in the bank, you burn it. You don't work as hard, and you aren't as creative about how to best get things done to maximize success. Most companies with millions and millions in funding waste it all and fail trying to figure out how to put it to work.

We leveraged being capital efficient and broke as a competitive advantage to think outside of the box, to innovate, and to make sh*it happen out of necessity. Heck, if we didn't, our wives would have probably left us or we could have lost our houses and everything we owned.

When you are about to lose everything you've got, it creates a sense of urgency for you to do whatever it takes to survive and thrive. You have no other option than to climb the wall, go around it, or dig a hole under it.

So instead of raising millions in funding, cherish being broke and bootstrapped. Spend all your time working with customers, developing products that maximize their results, and solving their biggest problems. Keep delivering solutions that customers love using and buying and continue to make them better and better.

Lean and mean will keep you innovating and focused on delivering for the only group of people who matter— your customers.

The best way to do this? Focus on creating a limitless outlook and work ethic no one can ever beat.

5

Go All Out

In life, you have three choices. Give up. Give in. Give it your all.

To become the best that you can be, you have to be dedicated to putting in the work. I'm talking about investing thousands of hours of your time over years and years to become the best you can be at what you do. There are no shortcuts and no guarantees.

To become the fastest, the smartest, the richest, and the best of the best, it will require you to put in the work every day, over long periods of time. You need to do this even when the excitement and novelty have worn off, leaving you in a dark place on the grind while everyone else is out of the office and enjoying life. This will be extremely hard to do in today's world of immediate gratification.

If you want to build a multimillion-dollar startup you have to put in the work. If you want to have an amazing relationship with your partner, you have to put in the work. If you want to make seven figures in sales, you have to put in the work. There is no way to sugarcoat this.

Yes, things may go faster than expected but it still takes time and effort repeated over long periods of persistence. A farmer cannot plant a tree and expect it to grow into the largest, most powerful tree in the world in a day. Farmers understand that when they plant anything, it will take time, patience, water, sunshine, and the right amount of effort to generate results.

You just have to want it and work for it. Change your mindset to enjoy the process along the way. Ask yourself (before you do anything) am I willing to invest 1,000 hours into mastering this and working on this every day to become the best that I can be? Ensure you are willing to do what it takes to become a true expert and top performer that generates top results at your craft.

IF IT WERE EASY, EVERYONE WOULD DO IT

I refer to this saying and concept daily. Whenever I don't want to get up to start work before the sun rises or keep grinding on sales or building the software when the sun sets and the office is empty, I just keep telling myself that if it were easy, everyone would do it.

The reason 99 percent of people aren't doing it is that it is the hardest, most exhausting, and immediately unrewarding thing to do. That being said, if you just keep at it, stay motivated, surviving, and thriving by fighting hard through the tough times, the good times are right around the corner.

BE READY TO WORK HARDER
THAN ANYONE ELSE

Wake up every day with the mindset that you will have to work harder, longer, and smarter than everyone else to achieve the results that you want to achieve.

Wake up every day with the mindset that you are going to have to hustle every second for what you want in this life.

If it comes easier and is less work for you, then that's great!

The reason why salespeople and entrepreneurs fail is that they always underestimate the amount of hard work, time, capital, and effort it takes to succeed. If you wake up every day knowing you are going to have to work your a$s off, you will never be let down.

You also must have a positive, can-do-whatever-it-takes attitude for any task, problem, or challenge that needs to be completed each day to take you to where you want to go.

Wake up every day with a relentless mindset to accomplish your goals and dreams.

DEVELOP A STRONG PAIN THRESHOLD

Becoming a seven-figure salesperson (or whatever success *you* want in life) is not for everyone. You need to have a high pain threshold.

Your days, weeks, and months will be filled with a lot of hard work and pressure. You will become stressed out and will be faced with constant challenges, failures, and opportunities. If you are wired and highly driven to make it happen, then you can do it. You just need to integrate the tolerance for a high pain threshold.

You will need to develop an ability to not give up unless you are forced to and have an insane amount of persistence and tenacity to keep going.

Whether that's prospecting, pitching, following up, or closing the number of deals that you need to generate seven figures in sales, you can do it if you put in the work. Stay tenacious and fight through any difficult challenges you encounter. As you endure pain and push through it, your threshold will become stronger.

YOU CAN'T BEAT SOMEONE
WHO NEVER GIVES UP

In life, you have three choices.

Choice #1: Give up.

Choice #2: Give in.

Choice #3: Give it your all.

You get to choose but I recommend going with option number three. You will never regret giving it your all, even if you fail. Plus, if you never quit, you will never fail.

It's amazing to find out what happens and who you become when you don't give up.

My father always told me that you don't quit. If you are going to do something, then you have to give it your all and try to become the best at it. The person who never gives up will always beat the person they are competing against.

Never f*cking quit or give in. EVER!

"Stay humble, stay hungry, and always be the hardest working person in the room."

- Dwayne "The Rock" Johnson

The life you want, the marriage you want, and the family you want are going to be fueled by the products and services that you can sell. This book gives you the habits required to truly win it all.

Dwayne "The Rock" Johnson had it right with the quote above. The only way to maximize your success is to give 110 percent. You need to totally and completely commit everything you have to go all-in. If not, then you shouldn't start in the first place.

Become utterly focused on your goals and relentlessly disciplined with executing the activity to achieve them, despite any external or internal circumstances you face.

HUSTLE BEATS TALENT WHEN TALENT DOESN'T HUSTLE

If you want to live like no one else lives, you better work like no one else works.

Hustle will always beat talent when talent doesn't hustle.

I also believe talent is created from the hustle. Even if you know people who are naturally talented, hustle will eventually beat them and win in the game of life.

Everything in life is a marathon, not a sprint. Be prepared to work your a$s off for a very long time before you achieve success.

HAVE A 10-20-30 YEAR MINDSET OF HUSTLE

Give it your all on execution. This way you will never be let down.

Everyone else quits because they think success will be achieved faster than it is. Winners anticipate. Losers react.

Losers react to failure because they didn't adequately prepare to win the long game so they quit.

Train for the marathon and execute daily on that marathon. Anticipate the long, hard, brutal grind and repetitive failure you will face.

Never quit. Then you will win big. If it happens sooner than you think, you just won the game of life faster.

Sales success is never owned. It is rented. And the rent is due every day.

Don't forget that when you think you are not replaceable.

Let me tell you loud and clear. You are replaceable.

I know it hurts hearing me say that.

Heck, even I'm replaceable as the CEO and Founder of Seamless. AI; I think about it every day.

The only way I get to stay in my spot is if I pay the piper.

- I owe rent every day.
- I owe rent to my customers.
- I owe rent to my users.
- I owe rent to my team members.
- I owe rent to my investors.
- I owe rent to my fans.
- I owe rent to my supporters.

Rent is due every day.

Get up and go pay rent today and prepare to pay it every day for the long road to success.

CREATE YOUR OWN LUCK BY COMMITTING

You create your own luck through the amount of work and commitment you put into your job. You can accomplish massive success by having the attitude and work ethic to do whatever it takes to succeed. The majority of the most successful people in the world are also the hardest-working people who invest long hours into their work.

Treat putting in the work and working hard as your best friends because they will eventually empower you to rise above problems and misfortunes. They will increase your confidence and give you the skills and experience you need to soar.

This hard work ethic, commitment, and optimistic mindset to do whatever it takes will also be viewed favorably by other people you interact with. People who work hard and are successful attract other like-minded people, which can help you, grow a network of like-minded professionals.

DEVELOP AN EXCEPTIONAL HABIT OF CONSISTENT ACTION

Don't do things sporadically to hit your goals. Instead, practice the art of persistence and endurance.

It's easy to get excited and enthusiastic about a new goal or idea. It's very hard to work every single day to accomplish it. This is what I call executing daily persistence and endurance.

Doing something daily separates the masses from the classes. It separates the top one-percent achievers from the rest of the pack. If you look at anyone who has had massive success, you will find a work ethic that got them where they are today.

Look at Salesforce CEO Marc Benioff, Amazon CEO Jeff Bezos, actors like Leonardo DiCaprio or Ben Affleck, companies like Facebook or Slack, athletes like Michael Jordan, the late Kobe Bryant, LeBron James, and Tom Brady. They all worked hard and put in the work every day for more than a decade. It's persistence and endurance over long periods of time that separate the winners from the losers.

Enthusiasm is great but execution daily over long periods of time with persistence and endurance will ensure you achieve success.

Develop the exceptional habit of consistent daily action repeated over decades.

Become utterly relentless and unreasonable with your focus on achieving your conquest.

MAKE MOVES, NOT EXCUSES

If it's important, you will find a way. If it's not important, you will find an excuse

Every time I want to accomplish something but I can't hit my goal, it's because I am not making the sacrifices, putting in the work, researching the best strategy, or executing my plan flawlessly without deviation.

For example, I love to bio-hack my body. One of my life goals is to get down to 7.5 percent body fat, just to personally say I did it.

I want to do this for myself, not to compete with anyone else. I don't care about any accolades or awards. I just want to develop the discipline required in my health, diet, and daily workout routines to pull off something that 99 percent of the global population doesn't accomplish.

In the pursuit of this goal, I know I can lose two to three pounds of weight per day if I intermittently fast and only have one whole-food plant-powered meal at 2 p.m. This means I don't eat anything before that meal and I don't eat anything after that meal. In the intermittent fasting world this is known as one meal a day (OMAD). I've been doing it for years, having only one to two meals per day, ideally between 1 and 2 p.m. and another around 5 or 6 p.m.

If I follow this fasting plan and eat a whole-food meal, not garbage like fast food, I can literally lose up to 10 pounds in four to five days. I've got the data. I've lost as much as 15 pounds in one week. Now I am not saying that this is the right thing to do and I am not a doctor. I am just sharing with you my journey to testing different inputs and outputs that lead to weight loss.

Whenever I am tracking what I eat, when I eat, how much I workout, etc., and jump on the scale and it doesn't move or goes in the wrong direction, I get pissed off then I look at my data.

The data tells me that I overate for dinner, ate too early for my first meal, ate three meals instead of one or two — you name it. It's very difficult to execute the plan flawlessly.

Whenever you are not hitting a goal, it's because you aren't putting in the work and sacrifices to make it happen. Every time I gain weight, skip the gym or eat like sh*t, I am telling myself that my goal is not that important and it's okay to not accomplish it.

This health hacking has been a wild journey but I know even if I fail or make excuses, I get up and try to do it smarter again the next day. I constantly remind myself of this critical habit to put into place.

You have to ask yourself, how important is the big goal you have? What are you willing to sacrifice to reach it? What are the steps needed to get started?

Your ability to make moves toward that goal will bring you out of a pit of despair, excuses, and help you to overcome paralysis by analysis for good.

"WORK SMARTER, NOT HARDER" IS BULLSH*T

This old adage is so wrong for so many reasons. It tries to make people feel good about finding the easy way out and the easy answers in life. It preaches, "Skip all the hard work and skip all the struggles to achieve your goals and dreams."

Let me reassure you, to accomplish your goals and dreams, it will take everything out of you and more hard work than you can ever imagine. There are no shortcuts.

The real payoff comes from working as hard AND as smart as you possibly can.

WORK LIKE HELL

I love this Seven Figure Sales Success Principle from Elon Musk. I have always worked 14 to 18 hours every single day, so I can easily relate to what Elon is reiterating.

This principle is one I have always believed in and executed on to generate seven figures in sales. Elon does an even more incredible job of highlighting the habit so I have just shared it word for word below:

"I mean you just have to put in 80 to 100 hour work weeks every week. This improves the odds of your success. If other people are putting in 40-hour work weeks and you are putting in 100-hour workweeks, then even if you're doing the same thing, you know that you will achieve in four months what it takes them a year to achieve."

His math makes a lot of sense.

COMPLACENCY KILLS CHAMPIONS

Once you're at the top of your game you CANNOT slow down and stop training to keep the trophy. Never take your foot off the gas!

You may think it's time to ease up and take a break, but the minute you become complacent, someone will be there to knock you off the top of the mountain.

Just ask boxer Mike Tyson, wrestler Ronda Rousey, and mixed martial art fighter, Conor McGregor.

Don't be a former sales champion who gets knocked out.

Always be hungry. Always be hustling to prove why you're #1.

SUFFER NOW AND LIVE THE REST OF YOUR LIFE AS A CHAMPION

This quote and seven-figure habit from Muhammad Ali embodies everything I am trying to teach you throughout this book.

Here is the reality: "I hated every minute of training, but I said, "Don't quit. Suffer now and live the rest of your life as a champion."

I refer back to this quote and picture all the times I wanted to quit or give up early. Whether I wanted to quit at work, at trying to be the best leader, or at trying to be the best husband or family member, I realized now is the time to put in the work and suffer.

Here is why: Every day that you throw in the towel early and quit on your goals and dreams to go home and relax, there is someone out there staying on the floor, still putting in work, still making calls, still sending emails, still customizing social touches, delivering more pitches, and closing more sales. Someone will use every second to train and get better.

One day, you are going to meet that person in a deal or in a pitch, and you will lose, all because they continued to suffer and put in the work.

You need to put in more effort, more money, more sacrifice, more training, more sweat, more tears, more blood, more capital, and more energy than anyone.

Go all out to beat the person staring back at you in the mirror along with your competition staring off in the distance at you.

Don't quit. Suffer now and live the rest of your life as a champion.

YOU AREN'T A F*CKING CANDLE, YOU AREN'T GOING TO BURN OUT

When people tell you not to work so hard, you are going to burn out, don't listen to them. You are not a candle. There is no way that you can burn out.

Whoever came up with this bullsh*t motto wanted a reason to not work hard.

You will never burn out unless you believe you can burn out. I want you to eliminate this false belief and made-up excuse that is used by people to help justify quitting and being lazy in life. You need to give it your all and you need to go at the pace that is perfect for you to make your goals and dreams a reality.

When people tell me I work too much, I tell them I am an iron triathlete at work. I will never get tired.

I can do this because, over the last 15 years, I've trained my mind, body, and brain to accomplish anything in this world I want to accomplish. They embody all the habits that I share with you in this book

Never worry about going too hard, working too hard, or going all-in and all-out to achieve your goals and dreams.

Everyone has their own pace and their own tolerance, so don't worry about what others tell you.

81

They are telling you to "Watch out, slow down, and be careful" because they quit on themselves, and their families. Do whatever it takes to make their dreams a reality.

FOLLOW UP AND FOLLOW THROUGH

To maximize your success in sales, business, life, job hunting, finding a partner, raising millions in funding, or generating millions in sales, you need to become an expert at following-up and following-through with the people who will help you get there.

A prominent 2019 sales study states that 48 percent of salespeople never follow up with a prospect.

- 25 percent of salespeople make a second contact and stop.
- 12 percent of salespeople make only three contacts and stop.
- Only 10 percent of salespeople make more than three contacts and two percent of sales are made on the first contact.
- Three percent of sales are made on the second contact.
- Five percent of sales are made on the third contact.
- 10 percent of sales are made on the fourth contact.
- 80 percent of sales are made on the fifth to twelfth contact.

The moral of the story is, don't give up. *"Follow-up and follow-through." The numbers don't lie.*

IF YOU WANT TO BE SUCCESSFUL, YOU HAVE TO PREPARE FOR SACRIFICE

Everyone wants to make a lot of money, get all the delicacies that are out there, and showcase it all over social media.

The problem is everyone wants to be a success, but only a small fraction wants to put in the hard work and sacrifice to make it happen.

Anyone can launch a company, but can you go 12 to 36 months without making any money because you invested every dollar of your life savings into the company.

This is what I had to do when I launched Seamless.AI. I became a millionaire using the product, then decided I wanted to go all-in to help professionals globally accomplish the same.

When I launched Seamless, no one knew who I was or would invest in me so I had to take nearly $1 million of my own cash and put it into funding the company.

For the next 12 months, I worked seven days a week, 8 to 14 hours a day, and paid myself zero salary.

Then, for the next year, I worked seven days a week, 14 to 18 hours a day, and paid myself the equivalent of $30,000.

The following year, I was finally able to afford to give myself a bonus and got to pay myself the equivalent of $40,000.

During those three years, I hired people who were critical to helping me grow the business. But they lied, cheated the system, and stole from me. I almost went bankrupt multiple times.

On top of all of this, I was traveling around the country pitching hundreds of venture capitalists (VC) to try and raise funds. I joined a VC portfolio group and had to move to Newark, New Jersey where I lived and worked out of an apartment studio next to Amazon (who invested in us).

My wife barely got to see me because, for months, I'd be stuck in Newark, grinding seven days a week for the company.

I didn't have a lot of money at the time so I would constantly drive back and forth from Newark, NJ to Ohio and back again.

Success looks awesome and everyone wants it, but virtually no one wants to eat all the sh*t every day to get there.

It's a lot of hard work (more than you can ever imagine).

It's a lot of sacrifices (more than you can ever calculate).

It's a lot of challenges (more than you can count).

Just be prepared for this.

Too many people fail because they underestimate how difficult it will be. If I can help prepare you for those challenges, you too can be successful.

I don't regret all the work and sacrifice I put in to accomplish everything I wanted to accomplish. It just took a lot of hard work and sacrifice that 99.9 percent of people can't endure.

If you are prepared and ready for this, then let's do it!

GO ABOVE AND BEYOND

The fastest way to make more money and get promoted is to give more than what is expected of you — in your job, for your prospects, to your partner, and for your family.

Whether you put in the minimum amount of work or the maximum amount of work, you're still working the same amount of time. Might as well make the most of it. For example, I can go to the gym and, during a 60-minute time period, I can burn 250 calories walking on a treadmill, or I can do a high-intensity workout and burn 600 to 750 calories. Either way, I just invested 60 minutes of my time to improve my health so I can either make it a great workout or a sh*tty workout. The time investment to do 250 calories or 600 to 750 calories is the same.

You might as well go all out and give it your all during whatever time you commit to accomplishing the task at hand to maximize the return on investment.

If you are headed into work on a Monday, you can have the mindset that you are going to capitalize on the day, get a ton of work done, and crush it. Or you can have the mindset that you hate Mondays, you don't want to do anything, and you sit there bored all day. Both options require the same amount of time so you might as well give it your all.

The same goes for spending time with loved ones, family, and friends. If you are going to commit the time with these people, go all out and give more than what is expected of you. Don't put in the bare minimum. You are already committed to going all-in with that commitment.

Applying this habit to family and friends was actually the hardest for me because I wanted to be all-in, giving it my all for my prospects, my customers, and my employees. When it came to taking time off from work to spend with family and friends, I hated it. I would half-a$s it, not be present, waste time on my phone half working on the business while at a family event.

Then I woke up and realized my family and my partner Danielle hated that I would give everything I had to the business but not to family and friends. So I decided to wake up and go all out with them as well. Now when I'm with them, I am 100 percent WITH them and live in the moment rather than tapping away at my laptop while half-listening. By doing so, my relationship with my wife, family, and friends has never been better.

The same goes for your prospects too. Give more than what is expected of you to your prospects. Over-deliver during the sale process. Over-deliver after the sale. Over-deliver in service.

Additionally, give more than what is expected of you at work. If you want to get promoted, get a bonus, get paid more, and have everyone at work love you, be the person who always gives more than what is expected — to your customers, to your employees, to your bosses, to your C-Suite, and to your company culture.

I always know who will always do their best every day to maximize the success of my company at Seamless versus the ones putting in minimum effort. Guess who are the ones getting promoted and getting bonuses the most? The ones who always give more than what is expected. I hope that person is you, and I hope you never take your foot off the gas.

Guess who are the ones getting promoted and getting bonuses the most? The ones who always give more than what is expected.

6

Never F*cking Quit

Giving up on your goal because you had one setback is like slashing the other tires on your car because you got one flat. You would NEVER do that. Get OVER it, and don't ever, ever, give up.

To continue maximizing your success, you need new ideas, insights, and strategies. You cannot get better if you close your mind to advice or feedback from people who can make you better. Always listen to them and aggressively tune out that nasty little voice in your head. You know, the one that tries to rationalize why you're not good enough, why you can't make it, and all the other limiting beliefs that hold you back if you let them. That little voice will infect you with doubts about your ability to succeed to the level you want to reach.

Shut those voices down after recognizing them for what they are — small obstacles that you address then move past.

Of course, you automatically face fears before taking risks, whether it's diving off a cliff or signing a new deal. Learn to capture that energy and defuse it or power forward so that voice can instead empower you to achieve more.

EMBODY A GROWTH MINDSET

You need to genuinely believe you are still at the beginning of your growth, not the end.

This includes your career, your job, your skills, and all facets of your life — professionally and even personally.

If you believe you are at the beginning of your growth, you will stay absolutely committed to continuously advance your capabilities with speed, agility, and commitment.

Embody a growth mindset forever. No matter the job, age, background, you are at the beginning of your journey.

DON'T LET A GOOD OR BAD ECONOMY STOP YOU FROM SUCCESS

Many readers like you will let a good or a bad economy hold them back from getting started on a big goal or dream. Before you make that mistake, remember that some of the most iconic companies in the next decade will be launching during challenging economic times (due to COVID19).

Just look at some of the innovative startups were founded in the last recession (2007-10):   .

Uber
Airbnb
Slack
Pinterest
WhatsApp
Square
Venmo

This alone goes to show you can become a success and accomplish all of your goals and dreams regardless of the state of the economy. Just imagine what the world would be like without these incredible companies.

Learn from their founders' examples. You are unstoppable. Just do it.

YOU CAN LEARN ANYTHING YOU NEED TO ACCOMPLISH IN THIS LIFETIME

If there is something I want to do, I just have to learn how to do it. I just have to model the plan and follow the recommendations of experts before me who have already accomplished what I want to do.

If you want to maximize sales, you can buy books to teach you everything about maximizing sales (like *The Seven Figure Sales System*—the 15 book series our company has written to help you earn seven figures fast!)

If you want to maximize sales, you can buy courses that will teach you everything you need to learn those techniques.

If you want to maximize sales, you can hire coaches and mentors to hold you accountable every day to hit your targets.

Paying the experts pays off.

Think about this: You have a tooth-ache and you need to see the dentist. They tell you it's going to cost $1,000 to pull your tooth. You then ask how long it will take and they tell you it should only take five minutes. Maybe you think, "Wow! $1,000 for five minutes is insane.That's so expensive!"

Then your dentist says, "Well, I can take 30 hours if you want, but that would be pretty painful."

I'd rather pay for the answer or solution to my biggest pain or problem and implement that solution right away instead of wasting days, weeks, months, or even years trying to find the answer the hard way. The same concept should apply to your dreams and goals.

For example, when I wanted to master sales, I bought 250 sales books and read them from cover to cover. This helped me learn everything I needed to know to maximize sales and launch multiple seven-figure startups, which eventually led to me launching Seamless.AI.

Stop wishing it were easier, and start wishing you were better. Don't wish for fewer problems. Wish for more expertise.

OPERATE LIFE IN A CONSTANT STATE OF OPTIMIZATION

Technology is always changing. The world around you is always changing. The only thing we know is certain in this life is that everything around you from your relationships to your job to your surroundings is in a constant state of chaos and flux.

You have to constantly be changing and optimizing to improve and get better every day and to keep up with the world around you.

Find, test, and execute new ways to maximize your personal and professional life.

Whether it's Day 1 or Day 3,679, continue to work hard, think, operate, and execute as hungrily as you did when you first started. Always look to find more cost-effective, better ways, to find and close more sales.

Learn how you can do it bigger, better, smarter, and faster.

SELF-EDUCATE AND INSPIRE DAILY

You need to invest time in self-education and self-motivation every day.

This can be reading a book, listening to an audiobook, watching a special training course, watching an inspiring motivational video, reviewing a book summary, watching a documentary, or reading a new article or blog that teaches you something to get better at your job in sales, entrepreneurship, marketing.

You are either moving forward towards your goals every day or you are moving backward daily. You get to decide.

If you put in the work every day to improve your education and motivation, you will achieve massive success. It is not a matter of "if" but a matter of "when."

Keep learning and staying motivated every single day.

Every challenge you overcome that you fear the most then overcome will create opportunity. You just have to do it.

ALWAYS BE CURIOUS

The person who always exudes curiosity, and experiments the most, wins.

Did you know that inventor Thomas Edison had more than 950 experiments before coming up with the lightbulb?

The best people, inventors, innovators, actors, athletes, and entrepreneurs all experimented often, failed many times, and remained curious to try again so they could optimize from failure.

Don't be afraid of being curious or finding a better way to do something. Don't be afraid of failing or experimenting to achieve greatness in sales and in life.

FAIL FORWARD TO GET BETTER

You need to get excited about the fact that you will fail multiple times on your way to seven-figure sales success. But you need to fail-forward, using failure as an opportunity to learn and improve—not give up. Just like Edison.

I came from the digital marketing world where everything is an A/B split test. You try one thing, you see the results. You try another thing, you see the results. Then you identify what generates the best outcome and keep trying to improve that variable.

Similarly, you have to stay in this constant state of optimization where failure is just a learning experience to propel you forward on your journey. I don't even mentally comprehend failure. I just see it as data to use so that I can optimize my efforts and my work and my activity to get to where I want to go.

BE OPEN TO COACHING

The habit that separates winners from the losers is coachability. Don't limit yourself to what you've learned, believed, or accomplished in the past. A person who is highly coachable but less skilled and educated can still outcompete other smarter, more skilled individuals.

You need to condition your brain to always get better and to do something smarter. Never say, "This won't work for me."

When an expert, mentor, coach, or boss tries to teach you something new that you can apply to maximize your results, resist saying "I know this already." You should focus on asking,

"What can I learn from this right here, right now, to further augment my results?"

Do you see the difference there?

One belief system says:

"I know this already. I don't need to pay attention, listen, or try to learn."

The better belief system says:

"What can I learn from this right now to improve my results and maximize my success?"

Every day, I wake up hungry, humble, and eager to be the hardest-working person in the room. I am searching for that one needle in the haystack that can fundamentally help my company positively impact a billion people.

When I was an 18-year-old in college, I had so much success, I thought I was the smartest and greatest entrepreneur in the world. With my second company called Enmobile, we were so damn egotistical because of all of our success from the first company, so we decided to not listen to a word these advisors said.

We hired 30 to 50 people because we wanted to show the world what smart entrepreneurs we were.

We got 10,000 square feet of office space to show the world what smart and great entrepreneurs we were.

We spent 14 hours a day working on the press to get the recognition to show the world what smart and great entrepreneurs we were.

In reality, we should've just listened to our mentors who were multi-millionaire experts. These people built and sold multiple companies and they had seen and done this over and over again. Unfortunately, we were too cocky and too full of ourselves to listen. We didn't embody a growth mindset.

You see how that story ended.

You have to have an open mindset and an eagerness to learn and apply what you learn, despite any knowledge you have gained in the past.

INVEST IN MENTORSHIP

If you are stuck in your conquest to success, that is okay. All you need to do is get out there and find the people who can help you get to where you want to go.

Tony Robbins says, "If you want to achieve success, all you need to do is find a way to model those who have already succeeded!" In other words, whatever you want to accomplish in life, there are experts and people out there that can help you. All you need to do is go find them and pay them to coach, train, or mentor you.

Yes, this will cost money but what is the true cost of not getting into the Seven Figure Club? Let's say you want to make $1 million a year in sales and right now you are at $100,000 so you decide to look for some help. You agree to pay an expert,

$10,000, $25,000, or even $100,000 to coach and mentor you on how to get there. The true cost of not making a million dollars this year is this:

$1,000,000

-$100,000

= $900,000 (The opportunity cost)

Anything more cost-effective than $900,000 to get you to generate $1 million in sales is worth the investment.

Heck, I've bought books for $20 that have helped me make an extra $100,000, $250,000, or $1 million. You don't need to invest $500,000. You can even just invest in buying books or training programs. They are out there. Consume their content; buy their books; buy their training; buy their technologies.

BECOME A "LEARNPRENEUR"

This is a word I just made up. Effectively, instead of solely being an entrepreneur or a salesperson, which is who you are at your core already, you need to become a reading and learning machine.

Someone has written or taught about anything you want to accomplish in this life.

The more knowledge and expertise you gain from reading books, taking courses, doing Masterminds, studying experts, and getting advice from mentors, the more you will most likely earn.

Learning everything about anything you want to achieve is the fastest way to accomplish and achieve the dreams you have to succeed.

LEVERAGE "JUST-IN-TIME" (JIT) LEARNING

Just-In-Time Learning is the act of only studying and learning things that you can use and apply today to maximize your potential.

It means that you do not waste time reading or studying topics that you can't put to use right away. The human brain will forget about what you study if it isn't applied immediately. You will not retain the majority of the things that you learn or study unless it can be applied to accomplishing your goals and dreams right now.

For example, I am going all-in on building a real-time search engine. Wasting any time on learning anything that doesn't build that business is a complete waste of effort, for right now. One of my other big goals is to have a real-estate portfolio of 1,000 properties. The problem with that goal is that all of my capital and money are invested in Seamless.

Instead of spending Saturday and Sunday studying how to invest in real estate, I am investing all of my just-in-time learning and personal development on building my tech startup Seamless.AI. By maximizing the success of Seamless, one day that will allow me to invest heavily in building a diverse real estate portfolio.

Right now all my JIT learning needs to go to maximize the success of my company.

If it's a goal or dream that you want to achieve in the future and not within the next 30 to 90 days, don't start studying it today. The effort will be wasted and have minimal impact. Learn and study what you can apply today.

ENCOURAGE CRITICISM AND CREATE FEEDBACK IDEA LOOPS

To maximize your success, you want to always look for productive criticism, feedback, and ideas to get better from others. Conducting an accurate self-audit is so important yet so difficult to do. We all assume too many things to be true (by that, I mean factual) without enough data or sufficient basis in the belief. A well-thought-out review or critique of whatever you're doing is as valuable as gold.

Usually, your co-workers or peers know what's wrong or how you can improve but they don't want to tell you because they don't want to offend you or hurt you. This does not mean they are always right but more often than not, they are.

It is important to have a feedback loop from your peers, managers, customers, and prospects to understand what you have done and how you could be doing it better.

Constantly ask yourself "Is this the best possible way to achieve the outcome I want?" I like to leverage the mindset that I am wrong with this idea or thought and work across the company to validate or invalidate that assumption. If I can be wrong less frequently, then I am on the right path to success.

Pay close attention to negative criticism and feedback. Instead of ignoring it and letting your feelings get hurt, you have to listen to it very carefully and respectfully. Learn from the feedback and figure out how you can adjust your actions and behavior to maximize your success, results, and positive contributions you can make to the company.

I am still not perfect at getting negative feedback and optimizing perfectly on it but I believe it's really important to solicit negative feedback from people who have your best interest in mind.

PICTURE ONE PERSON YOU CAN HELP

Anything that you want to do in this life, you just need to ask yourself, "Can I help just one person?"

I used to let fear and other people's opinions, thoughts, and fears hold me back from accomplishing my goals and dreams. Then I had an epiphany. If I can help just one person, then it's worth it.

While our software affects the lives of more than 100,000 people — and growing! — I imagine a single person like myself that is frustrated at the lack of data they need and want. Then, I work to solve that person's problem.

Making that connection makes the solution more than checking an item off your to-do list. It makes it personal and relatable.

If I help that one person, then I find the answer to assist thousands of others with the same problem. But boiling it down to a real or imagined person who faces their fears makes it easier to envision how to get to the finish line. It also makes it about more than your emotions.

If it helps, create a narrative to help you or your team to move past the obstacle — no matter how scary it is — to change one person's life.

You will find it is a lot less terrifying when you shift the focus.

ALWAYS SEEK IDEAS FROM EVERYONE

Ask for ideas from your prospects, your customers, your employees, your network, and your mentors. Be constantly on the lookout for ideas that are simple, differentiated, and have the potential to maximize your success. You can always find new products, features, or services to sell. You can always find better ways to do something.

Always be on the search for new ideas and then test those ideas patiently with data.

PAY ATTENTION AND ACTIVELY LISTEN

When you are in meetings with co-workers, peers, investors, customers, or prospects, give them your undivided attention when they are speaking with you. With all the distractions nowadays, it's very difficult to give your undivided attention to everyone.

That being said, you need to.

No one likes to meet with someone who multi-tasks and they have to repeat themselves to get their point across.

Give respect to others by giving them your full, undivided attention.

This habit is something I am working to improve every day.

Also, give at least one compliment a day. Imagine someone in your professional or personal life you would love to get praise from, and what it would feel like if you did.

Compliments are incredible and create a dopamine effect in the brain for not only the person receiving the compliment but also for the person giving it.

First, the person receiving the compliment feels amazing that their hard work and effort is having an impact. They will feel loved, appreciated, and thankful that it is getting noticed.

Second, the person giving the compliment gets to feel amazing by appreciating someone who is working so hard, trying to help change the world. They get to see how that compliment positively impacted someone, creating a reverse dopamine effect on the giver of the compliment.

Company-wide, during all of our "standup" meetings, I require every person to state what they did yesterday, what they are doing today, any blockers, and then kudos (a compliment) to a coworker for something awesome they did.

That creates a great sense of teamwork and reinforces that feedback can be positive, as well as constructive.

TAKE FEEDBACK AND RUN WITH IT

Feedback can be tough. Taking feedback can hurt, especially if it's critical.

But when someone points out a legitimate flaw in your beliefs or points out incorrect actions you are or aren't taking, they are not criticizing you. They are presenting a better alternative. Our ability to take feedback and apply it truly can make or break our careers.

Here's a shocker for you. There are some people who might know more than you.

Here's another shocker. You (and I) are not perfect.

I have one more for you. You (and I) can always get better. No. Matter. What.

Feedback can come from all sources — those above us, but also those more junior than us. Never discount it. With the right feedback, you can duplicate your results faster than if you go alone.

Now, is taking feedback easy? Not always.

Here's a trick I've learned. Write it down as it's happening. Get it out of your head. It slows the emotion, makes you less defensive, and you take some ownership in.

Then ask for examples of how to apply it. Write that out too.

You should be SEEKING feedback and applying where it makes sense.

"If anyone can prove and show to me that I think in error, I will gladly change it.. for I seek the truth"

–Marcus Aurelius

YOU NEVER LOSE IN LIFE, YOU EITHER WIN OR YOU LEARN

Do a postmortem review on every move you make.

Why did you win? Why did you lose? What did you do well?

In sales, I always ask myself, "What could be improved to increase my probability of winning the deal next time around?"

I NEVER want to say, "There is nothing else I could have done."

This should signal a red flag in my mind–my bullsh*t meter going off telling me I couldn't answer, "What could be improved to increase the probability of me winning the sale?"

There is *always* something I can do better on every deal, whether I win or lose the sale.

Be brutally honest about identifying what it is that could be improved.

Remember, if you improve 1 percent every day, by the end of the year, you will have increased your results by 260 percent (there are roughly 260 business days in a year).

If you improve by 2 percent every day, by the end of the year, you will have increased your results by 520 percent.

If you improve 3 percent every day, by the end of the year you will have increased your results by 780 percent.

The multiplier effect speaks volumes, and the data will always be teaching you something new.

REVEL IN THE DARK MOMENTS TO APPRECIATE THE STARS

It's always the darkest before the light.

I've made and lost millions in sales and entrepreneurship. Every time before making millions in sales was the worst period of my life.

But, I didn't quit. I believed that if I just kept fighting and optimizing, I would nail it.

If the past year was hard for you, I can relate.

I've been there over and over again, and this is for you.

Keep f*cking fighting.

Don't quit on me.

TURN I CAN'T INTO I CAN

You *can* do anything. Never say that you cannot do anything. This is a loser's mentality. A winner's mentality believes that they can do anything. A seven-figure sales producer's mentality believes they can do anything.

Whenever you think that you "can't" do something, repeat to yourself out loud "I Can Do Anything." Whenever I start saying "I can't" or when I start having negative thoughts about a big goal, task, or mission, I just start repeating out loud: "I can do anything."

It's a great mental reminder that there is nothing you cannot do in this world. Don't believe anyone — even yourself — that you cannot do something you truly want.

Adopt a positive and optimistic attitude about everything in life.

DON'T SWEAT THE SETBACKS

We have all made mistakes or encountered setbacks on our journey to maximize our success. Sometimes they're big. Sometimes they are small. Sometimes we make the same mistakes over and over again.

The one thing you need to understand, however, is that encountering setbacks and making mistakes is okay as long as you learn from them.

Don't spend too much time thinking about the mistake.

Analyze what went wrong.

Learn from the setback or mistake.

Apply the learning to maximize your growth.

Don't sweat the setbacks. Just keep going. Giving up on your goal because you had one setback is like slashing the other three tires in your car because you got one flat. You would NEVER do that. Get OVER it, and don't ever, ever, give up.

DON'T THINK ABOUT ASKING, JUST ASK

When I started in entrepreneurship and sales, I was afraid to ask people the important questions that would help me grow my business, increase sales, and maximize value to the customer.

Because I was new to sales and entrepreneurship, my fear of sounding "dumb" held me back from asking the questions that would have given me the answers to be successful. When I finally got over my fear and started asking those important questions to move my business forward, my revenue, sales, and income skyrocketed.

This one habit of "just ask" is so powerful and can change the trajectory of your success forever for the better.

GET EXCITED ABOUT FEAR AND REJECTION THEN AND RUN TO IT

Whenever I am scared or worried about the world hating my new product, the software we built, books we wrote, or social media posts, etc, I know I am doing new things and heading in the right direction.

I have trained my mind and body to get excited about fear and rejection and when I sense them, I force myself to run to it versus away from it.

This habit took me more than over a decade to master.

When you keep running towards fear and rejection by trying new things and executing ideas that you have never executed before, your brain will freak out and get scared about others hating the idea and rejecting you.

This comes from our brain's need for safety, love, and belonging like Abraham Maslow highlights in his hierarchy of needs.

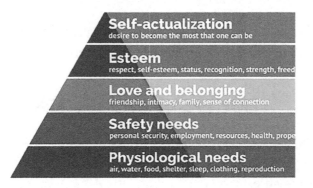

However, if you don't listen to your need for love, belonging, and safety, and instead try all the things that you have always dreamed of doing regardless of fear and rejection, you will become limitless.

Whether it's calling that prospect back on a deal you have been working on for months and need to close it by shooting a video to post on Linkedin, run towards it.

I was scared sh*tless to release the first book that I wrote and self-published. When we launched it with no marketing plan on the first day, we persisted, and it became a #1 new release and best-seller with the help of a last minute push over the finish line.

I was scared because I didn't know how to write. I didn't think I had anything to say. I didn't think anyone would care. I wasn't sure if anyone could be positively impacted etc. The list of fears went on and on.

You see, my brain was trying to shut me down in paralysis by analysis and use the fear of rejection to get me to quit and give up.

Tens of thousands of copies of my books have positively impacted people globally around the world. What if I didn't go forward with it because of fear?

The thing we fear the most never happens. And if it does, who gives a sh*t? You will learn from it and try again smarter the next time.

FIGHT FEAR WITH ACTION

Fear equals false events appearing real. I have killed more goals, dreams, projects, and aspirations because of fear than anything else in my life.

We fear that we won't be able to do it.

We have fear about what other people will think.

We fear losing time, money, or energy.

We fear getting hurt.

We fear losing loved ones.

We fear trying and then never being successful.

News alert. All these fears that we come up with within our heads are not true. These fears are considered, "False Events Appearing Real."

None of my fears ever came true, but quite the opposite.

The faster you can realize that fear, means you are headed in the right direction and you should use an action to destroy the enemy, "paralysis by analysis."

I was scared to share video content on LinkedIn and now have more than 1 million viewers per month.

I was scared to self publish my book, but it was such a great experience, we decided to write and publish 18 more.

I was scared to build Seamless.AI and now we help more than 100,000 salespeople, marketers, and entrepreneurs maximize sales with sales lists generated by Seamless.A.I.

Everything I have ever accomplished in this life, I was scared of doing.

The fastest way we can all work to overcome this fear is to realize that everyone else who was massively successful was also scared sh*tless and had to face immense FEAR to do what they did.

But they didn't let FEAR stop them. Neither should you.

You are going to run into obstacles, you are going to fail–especially if you're trying to generate massive results. But you have to do it anyway and test what may not be as successful as other things.

Whenever anyone tells you that it cannot be done, that is your signal to work harder.

Just remember, success is not final. Failure is not fatal. It's the courage to give it your all every day and do whatever it takes that counts.

Massive action will destroy any fear you have, and win the game, you have to take the game-winning shot regardless if it goes in.

Just take your shot.

Every day.
Every hour.
Every minute.
Every second.
Just take your shot.
Right now.
Not tomorrow.
Not next week.
Not next month.
Not next quarter.
Not next year.
Just take your shot.
Right now.

NEVER WAIT TO GET STARTED

It's never too late to get started and it's never too late to make your dreams come true.

Consider the career trajectories of these people who hit the reset button in their lives. I saw this example via an article recently:

At age 23, Oprah was fired from her first reporting job.

At age 24, Stephen King was working as a janitor and living in a trailer.

At age 27, Vincent Van Gogh failed as a missionary and decided to go to art school.

At age 28, J.K. Rowling was a suicidal single parent living on welfare.

At age 30, Harrison Ford was a carpenter.

At age 30, Martha Stewart was a stockbroker.

At age 37, Ang Lee was a stay-at-home dad, working odd jobs.

Julia Child released her first cookbook at age 39 and got her own cooking show at age 51.

Vera Wang failed to make the Olympic figure skating team, didn't get the Editor-in-Chief position at *Vogue*, and designed her first dress at age 40.

Stan Lee didn't release his first big comic book until he was 40.

Samuel L. Jackson didn't get his first movie role until he was 46.

Morgan Freeman landed his first MAJOR movie role at age 52.

Kathryn Bigelow only reached success for *The Hurt Locker* at age 57.

Just imagine how scared they were when they changed course to chase their dreams.

Whatever you dream, it's never too late to achieve it. You can do it.

Maximize Your Potential

To be successful in life, you have to do what's required, and you have to follow through. Pay the price today so you can pay any price tomorrow.

I love kicking off the morning with a win by jumping into action ahead of the sun. An early start helps me build momentum and achieve my goals throughout the day.

Of course, there are days I feel like beating my head against a wall. I can get stuck; I can't reach the right people; my product won't cooperate, or I simply don't make monumental progress with my business. When midday hits, I feel frustrated, demoralized and I start sniping at people.

Unless I prevent those days from happening at all.

While your attitude makes one hell of a difference, there are also some habits you can adopt to ensure every day is a productive day. Here are a few of my favorites that have helped me.

DEFINE YOUR "GUIDING LIGHT"

Before I work on anything, I ask myself four questions that are landmarks to my guiding light, (a.k.a. the things that guide all of the work that I do every day):

#1) Does this help me maximize my wealth?

#2) Does this help me maximize my health?

#3) Does this help me maximize my potential?

#4) Does this help positively impact 1 billion people?

If the answer to any of these four questions is yes, I move forward.

If the answer to any of them is no, I don't.

If the work doesn't align with my mission to help the world connect to opportunity and our vision to positively impact 1 billion people, I just won't let myself do it.

You need to define your guiding light, via the questions backed by your mission and vision for the time you have here in this world.

Focus on doing the things that maintain your integrity to execute the tasks aligned with your guiding light.

SAY NO TO THINGS THAT MOVE YOU AWAY FROM YOUR GOALS

You have to learn who to give your time to and how to say no to new tasks or requests from friends and family that will take you in the wrong direction— away from what you're trying to accomplish.

One of the best ways to do this is by keeping a calendar. Block out time for the most important tasks and it will allow you to easily and genuinely say no to others and tell them that you already have prior commitments that you have to stick to.

You will have to say no to more things than you say yes to, and you will just have to accept that people will not understand. People will be disappointed in you, and people will respond negatively. But it simply doesn't matter if the activities they are proposing will not allow you to reach your goals. You have to become an expert at saying no to distractions.

It's not easy; it's not fun, and it will be hard. This will force you to stay focused and say "yes" to the work that is required to accomplish your goals and dreams. And that is what is most important.

If you want to create long-term, permanent sales success habits in all aspects of your life, start small by completing little tasks every day and build from there. Celebrate the small wins every day towards your goal and they will all add up over time to big wins. Every major accomplishment was built by a collection of small accomplishments that accumulated over time.

How do you get started? Identify the good habits that are moving you towards your goals and double down on augmenting them. Identify the bad habits that are moving you backward and further away from your goals. Make a list of things you will stop doing that feed into these bad habits moving you away from your goals.

One example could be you want to lose weight but then you drink pop and eat fast food. Diet is 90 percent of losing weight so you need to make the right eating decisions to get where you want to go. One way to do this if you drink pop every day (which I recommend eliminating for a number of health reasons) is to only drink a cup on the weekend (limiting your intake). Double-down on the good and continue trying to eliminate the bad. Over time, this will compound to accomplish your goals.

A personal goal of mine is to socialize without ever having a drink (I don't ever want to decrease productivity or slow my brain down). Instead of going out for a drink on a Friday night, I can make tea and write one page for my book. This takes the new habit and replaces an old bad habit.

I keep an extensive list of good habits I am trying to develop and bad habits I am trying to remove every single day. And celebrating the completion of your daily new habits is a great way to maintain them throughout your hectic days, months, and years in sales.

Emotions create seven-figure success habits, not logic. That's why it's critical that you celebrate whenever you practice your new habit. There is a direct correlation between how you feel when you complete a habit and celebrate it and the likelihood that you will repeat that habit in the future. Positive reinforcements, accomplished thoughts, and upbeat celebrations will help reinforce those habits and make you feel successful.

The life you want, the family you want, the marriage you want, and the sales you want depending on the habits you build and the choices that you make every day. The great news is, you get to decide.

PRIORITIZE YOUR MOST IMPORTANT TASKS (MITS)

When you wake up, identify all the tasks you need to get done that day and prioritize them using a priority-execution roadmap. To make an impact, you need to rank your tasks with clarity and confidence. Focus on the activities that will generate the greatest return versus the ones that will have a minimal impact.

This concept not only applies to your personal growth and development, but also to your organization. I've actually used this exact approach to build multimillion-dollar businesses from the ground up.

Our team creates a product-priority roadmap, where we list everything we need to do in sales, marketing, customer success, operations, engineering, and recruiting — you name it.

For each division, we then create a priority-task roadmap where we list every single possible task that we need to work on. You can use something as simple as Google Sheets to list everything then score each task based on factors like revenue impact, usage, level of effort, and any other criteria that may be essential to your business.

By using a powerful task-prioritization framework, we can rank tasks objectively based on strategic criteria. Not all factors or criteria will hold the same weight so you will need to determine which factors are the most important for your organization.

You should collaborate with your team and have each member score your tasks and initiatives then take the average from the group to get your final scores.

For example, our task-priority roadmap for our sales operations team asks the following:

On a scale of 1-10 (10 being the greatest), how much does this task increase sales?

On a scale of 1-10 (10 being the greatest), how much does this task increase sales automation (automate manual tasks, remove clicks, remove manual data entry for sales team)?

On a scale of 1-10 (10 being the greatest), how much does this task increase security?

On a scale of 1-10 (10 being the greatest), how much does this task improve management's decision-making?

On a scale of 1-10 (10 being the greatest), what is the level of effort (number of hours) to complete this task?

Task Prioritization			
Items	Value	Effort	Priority score
Mobile app			95
Website redesign			83
Slack bot			28

Our sales operations team scores each of its tasks based on this prioritization roadmap so that all of their work is automatically prioritized based on what delivers the greatest value to the company.

If you are driving 100 miles per hour the wrong way to your destination (your goal), you will never get there no matter how fast you go.

Prioritizing your tasks every day ensures that you are working on the right things to get you to your destination.

The smartest seven-figure entrepreneurs, salespeople, marketers, and product developers all prioritize their tasks religiously and work on the most important tasks first.

I highly recommend you do the same and create this daily habit ASAP!

BREAK DOWN BIG PROJECTS INTO SMALL, EASY-TO-MANAGE-TASKS

When you want to work on a big project, make sure you break your big tasks into smaller, easy-to-manage assignments.

Before you get started, you will want to list out every little task that would add up to completing the big project. Make sure you think of the impacts on every department and person and go systematically through the process from A to Z as you try to cover all your bases. You don't want to leave out any details that could derail your plans at the last minute. By including your team, you can all contribute to the list.

This way, you break down your massive project into small, bite-sized tasks that are more manageable. It also makes more people accountable as they see themselves as part of the process.

After you list out all the items that need to get done to complete the big project, you can prioritize them all and get to work! Breaking the process down like this helps you set up realistic, but ambitious, timelines, and budgets.

Tackling a project this way also makes it feel more achievable and takes off the pressure of the unknown because it is all laid out in front of you.

NEVER SAY YOU DON'T HAVE TIME

"I don't have time" is a bullsh*t excuse that you tell yourself so that you can feel good about not going all-in to accomplish your goals and dreams.

Take advantage of this opportunity of a lifetime. The definition of opportunity is when luck meets preparation. Preparation is created by putting in the hard work. Now it's time for you to go all out, work hard, prepare, and capture this opportunity of a lifetime.

Everyone has time. If I was able to build a multimillion-dollar company at the age of 18 to 21 while in college full-time and if I was able to write 15 sales books while building a $1 million software search engine while also traveling every other week on the speaking circuit, then you can make the time to do whatever you want to do to make your goals and dreams a reality.

"I don't have time" is an excuse. The real thing you are saying is I don't want to make the sacrifice and commit the time required to bring this goal to fruition.

Of course, we all want to watch TV, go out on the weekends, hang out with friends and family, relax and enjoy life, and travel the world. But guess what? That isn't going to get you closer to accomplishing your goal.

There are more than 1,400 minutes in a day. That is plenty of time. You can wake up earlier, go to bed later, turn off the TV and skip going out with friends. I challenge you to audit every 15-minute time block that you have in your life and you will see that you have plenty of time that is being wasted on unnecessary stuff.

If there's something you want to learn and master, make the time. Instead of listening to the radio and news while you drive to work, which is bulls*t propaganda to keep you scared of life in the first place, listen to a course, listen to a book, listen to a podcast that gets you closer to accomplishing your goals.

Work on your goals on the weekend. I work seven days a week to accomplish my goals and dreams. God took off the seventh day because he created the world. He deserves one day off because he created mankind. Now I know I'm not a religious person but this is a great example. Wait until you've accomplished something massive before you take time off.

There's so much time in the world, you just have to commit to using every minute of it and putting in the work.

Stop lying to yourself. Find the time. It's out there, you just have to use it.

INVEST YOUR TIME WISELY

Whether you are just starting in sales or are a 10-year veteran at a company, you have to invest your time and resources wisely into maximizing your sales results output.

If you waste your time, capital, energy, and resources, your chances for success greatly diminish, and your odds of achieving success decrease rather than increase.

Ask yourself "Will this activity today result in filling my pipeline, booking more appointments or closing more deals?"

If not, I recommend that you stop those efforts.

Do only a few activities incredibly well and invest your energy and resources into the sales work that generates the sales results.

Avoid doing things and working on projects that don't maximize sales. Period.

FILL YOUR CALENDAR WITH NO EXTRA TIME (NET)

Develop a calendar packed with NET (No Extra Time).

You should be as productive as possible every single day and pack your calendar so full that you have no extra time to ever waste on it.

When you have extra time on the calendar, you waste it.

When you don't have any extra time on the calendar, you maximize it.

No Extra Time (NET) maximizes your NET sales, income, and revenue results.

Automate and outsource anything that isn't in your expertise OR costs a lower hourly rate.

I originally learned this at a young age from my father. He would never work on anything that didn't have to do with sales because his hourly rate with all the sales commissions and overrides on his team was around $500 an hour. Any hour he was spending not selling or closing deals for his company was being wasted.

When I launched all of my different companies, anything that was a very manual, tedious mind-numbing task I would outsource as well as anything dealing with manual labor outside of my domain expertise, etc.

Automate and outsource anything that isn't in your expertise OR costs a lower hourly rate. Track your metrics daily.

"If you can't measure it, you can't improve it!" Tracking your metrics daily will empower you to clearly see the impact of your work— positively or negatively. With that truth, you can make changes to better achieve your goals without letting emotions, fears or excitement take over.

SKILL-UP DURING TRAVEL

Whenever you are traveling, make sure you use this time to get better. Don't waste it.

When I am traveling for the holidays, I am reading books on how to get better.

When I am traveling for work on flights, I am either working, reading, or watching courses on developing new skills.

When I am driving anywhere, I am listening to new books on audio spanning sales, marketing, entrepreneurship, or leadership.

A lot of my friends watch movies or read magazines and waste the time.

If you want to become a seven-figure success, you have to squeeze the juice out of every second.

Always make the most out of your travel time to do more work or to skill up.

You never know when you will uncover that next big secret that changes your life forever for the better.

PAY FOR WIFI ON PLANES

It amazes me when my coworkers, peers, or friends travel with me and they aren't buying WiFi and working on the plane. If you want to make seven figures in sales or be ultra-successful in whatever you do, you need to squeeze in every minute you have available to work.

I would constantly coach my sales guy Mike or my video guy Mason, telling them that flying is the best time to crank as hard as possible on work. Fork over the $7 it costs to get WiFi and go for it. Even if you aren't in sales, the more you produce in your field and the more expertise you gain to become the #1 expert in your category, and the more you earn.

The first time I made more than $137,000 in sales commissions in one month and more than $1.2 million in one year, I was traveling 100 days a year and working from 5 a.m. to 10 p.m.

I would be working in Ubers, in airplanes, in airports, in restaurants, wherever I was traveling. Hell, I even bought a lap desk for the car and would use it in the front passenger seat so if I had long drives, I would work all the time while a colleague drove or I would just hire a driver to drive me because my hourly rate at the time was more than $575 an hour.

So just fork over the $7, buy the damn airplane WiFi and get to work there and wherever you are. Stop making excuses and making lazy your reality. Lazy won't make you rich. Working your a$s off and capitalizing on every second will.

LEVERAGE EVERY DECISION
WITH THE 80/20 RULE

The 80/20 rule is based on Pareto's Principle that states for just about everything that happens in the world, roughly 80 percent of the effects come from 20 percent of the causes. This concept started in 1895 when Italian economist Vilfredo noticed 80 percent of the land was owned by 20 percent of the population, no matter which country you visit.

Coincidentally, the richest 20 percent of the world's population control 82.7 percent of the world's income, although the numbers vary from country to country. In the U.S., the top 20 percent of earners have paid about 80 to 90 percent of federal income.

It also applies to engineering and computer science. For example, when Microsoft fixes the top 20 percent of the most-reported bugs, 80 percent of the related errors and crashes disappear. In coding, it is commonly known that 80 percent of a certain piece of software can be written in 20 percent of the total allocated time. Conversely, the hardest 20 percent of the code takes 80 percent of the time.

Overall, Pareto's Principle indicates that in any scenario, only about 20 percent of factors are critical and roughly 80 percent are insignificant.

According to the 80/20 rule, the input and output relationships do not balance out.

When I recommend you leverage your decisions with this formula, I mean you should use data to automate 80 percent of the decisions you need to make in sales to maximize speed, velocity and build your predictable, repeatable and scalable sales results. This is especially critical for any decisions that aren't of the utmost importance, like decisions that can be easily changed or reversed, and the ones that don't have any significant long-term consequences.

If you're good at following the trajectory of a decision, you can recognize quickly that you went in the wrong direction and redirect. This approach and high-velocity decision making will always be better than being slow to decide or take action.

For the remaining 20 percent of decisions (the ones that cannot be reversed or changed without severe long-term consequences), work with your people, customers, prospects, mentors, investors and all the data about the external and internal environment to make as great of a decision as possible.

These 20-percent decisions can make or break your company so move slowly, think fast, analyze all the data, and be smart with the decision. It can make or break your year in sales.

CUT YOUR DEADLINES IN HALF

However long you think a task will take, cut it in half. Force yourself to do more work in less time to get the goal accomplished faster.

Figure out the daily or hourly tasks and activities required for completion to get it done by the new deadline. Overcommit to the goal or task that you need to complete right now.

We always overestimate what we can do in an hour and under-estimate what we can get done in a day.

If you are truly committed to getting something done, focus on it with all your energy and push through until it is done. You will be surprised how quickly you will move ahead once you adopt this approach.

WORK SMART NOT JUST HARD

You can work hard but if you don't work smart, you'll work every day for the rest of your life. How do you work smart? You need to prioritize the work tasks that will have the greatest impact on moving you from where you're at today to where you want to go to achieve your goals and dreams.

For example, if your goal is to make $1 billion in sales, and you know that 80 percent of sales is prospecting, but you spend every single day of the week reading a sales book, you will never get to seven figures in sales because you're reading while you should be prospecting. The person who is out there prospecting 24/7 is going to get there.

You have to work smart and prioritize all of your tasks from the highest impact to lowest impact, and score everything you do every single day. Continuously ask yourself, "Is this the smartest, best thing that I can do today to get me from where I am to where I want to go to?"

CREATE SCORECARDS TO STAY ON TRACK

I highly recommend creating a scorecard to prioritize your daily tasks. Figure out your scoring criteria which determines how important a task is in the bigger picture of achieving your goals.

Maybe it's sales; maybe it's appointments; maybe it's sales leads; maybe it's level of effort. Score all of your tasks daily based on your goals and how each task will help you achieve your goals, then work on the tasks that have the greatest impact on driving your desired results.

I have a scorecard for marketing, customer success, product development, engineering, HR, etc. We score and prioritize every single task that we want to accomplish and we evaluate what will best help us achieve our goals and dreams — what will help us generate 1 million people making over $1 million in sales a year in the fastest way possible.

Most of my scorecards are made up of four to 10 different factors and I weigh each task differently depending on its impact. The weights can change from month to month, quarter to quarter, depending on what you're trying to accomplish.

Use the scorecard to identify your most impactful to least impactful tasks and score the tasks you complete each day. Then, you can see if your hard work is going toward the things that are generating the greatest results and the greatest return on your time.

If you work smart and hard, you won't have to work for the rest of your life, because you can earn a higher ROI in a shorter amount of time.

JOIN THE TOP 1%

Many people know what they need to do to achieve success in life but few actually follow through with it. This is mainly because it requires hard work, sacrifice, time, money, and the effort to do the things that we don't want to do.

We will never always be motivated and inspired to get to work but the top one percent, the best of the best, the people who make seven figures in sales, they get up and put in the work no matter what, every day. Regardless of how motivated and inspired you are, just get up and get to work today—right now.

To be successful in life, you have to do what's required, you have to follow through, you have to do those things that you know you need to be doing. Pay the price today so you can pay any price tomorrow.

MASTER THE ART OF DELEGATION

The only way to scale to millions in sales every year is to build, grow, and empower a team. Master the art and science of delegation.

I am a salesperson, entrepreneur, marketer, author, and product engineer. If I have any task that doesn't align with these four core areas, I outsource them.

For example, I automate all of my landscaping, grocery shopping, laundry, shopping, you name it. Anything that would waste my expertise or time that is a lower hourly rate I automate and outsource.

I recommend that you do the same because to generate or make seven figures, it is going to take all of your time, work, and effort to make happen. You cannot be wasting your time and capacity on things that don't maximize your potential.

If you don't have the money to automate and outsource these tasks no problem. Work to increase your income and then slowly automate all of these tasks.

You need to find the right experts, set your expectations, define milestones, establish KPIs and track performance daily, weekly, monthly, quarterly, and annually.

DO THE HARDEST THING FIRST EVERY DAY ON YOUR TO-DO LIST

We all have a massive to-do list made up of hard tasks and easy tasks. Out of the three to five things you need to get done today, do the hardest task that you are looking forward to the least, and knock it out. This will create so much momentum that you will become unstoppable during the day. You'll find yourself being able to complete those easier tasks even faster and simpler than before.

If you tackle and complete an easy task first, by the time you get to the hard task, it will never get done. Your day will be interrupted by unexpected intrusions or you will start congratulating yourself for working through most of your list and slack off.

Don't take your foot off the gas pedal.

Climb that mountain first thing and you will feel amazing. Then capture that energy to blow through the rest of your list and your day will be fulfilling and will take you one step — or more!! — closer to your goal.

On your to-do list, prioritize and complete the hard thing first, followed by the easy things.

IF YOU DON'T PRIORITIZE YOUR LIFE, SOMEONE ELSE WILL

You have to prioritize everything you need to do every single day and avoid distractions because if you don't, someone else will.

For example, if you have 15 to 18 hours in a day on a Saturday, and you have no plans to do any work, then your day is going to get filled up with things based on someone else's priority list instead of yours. What this means is, the priorities of others will now become your priorities, regardless of if they help you achieve your goals and your dreams and/or the ultimate goal of making more than seven figures in sales.

You need to prioritize your life before others do it for you. What are your goals, what are your dreams, and what do you need to accomplish in your life today? Make it happen before your calendar gets flooded with the priorities of others.

STOP THINKING AND START DOING

Paralysis by analysis—sitting there thinking about what you need to do, what you should do, what you want to do—will accomplish nothing.

The secret to getting ahead is to just get started and the secret to getting started is to break down your complex overwhelming tasks into small manageable tasks, then to complete the first one.

The more you just think, the less you do, but the more you do, the more you think and the more you get done.

Start executing and you won't be able to stop thinking because the thinking will come along with the action. But if you don't take action and you just sit there thinking then nothing will ever get done.

They say discipline weighs ounces while regret weighs tons. You will never be upset on your deathbed that you were disciplined, tried, then failed. But you will regret it if you never tried to accomplish what you wanted, by overcoming the pain of discipline, the hard work, and the fear of failure.

The secret to getting ahead is to just get started.

INACTION IS THE DEATH OF YOUR POTENTIAL

I've lost more deals and opportunities in my life because of inaction.

Don't let paralysis by analysis kill any future relationships, opportunities, or accomplishments.

Inaction occurs because we overthink taking action or don't want to put in the work and sacrifice to make it happen.

I've taken the most inaction not because I want to avoid putting in the work, but because I overthink if people will find value in what I am putting the work into.

That's the big definition of paralysis by analysis. Instead of just making it happen and taking the action to put whatever you want to accomplish in motion, you overthink it, don't do anything and then that big idea, strategy, or goal dies right then and there Don't let inaction kill your goals, dreams, and potential. Take action right now, figure the rest out later. Your life depends on it.

Don't let inaction kill
your goals, dreams,
and potential. Take
action right now,
figure the rest out later.
Your life depends
on it.

8

Find Solutions, Not Problems

When you assume responsibility for your failures and successes, you gain the clarity needed to see what is holding you back from being successful.

People don't care how much you know until they know how much you care. I remember someone telling me this when I started early in my sales career in the early 2000s and the saying still holds true to this day.

If you stink of sales commission breath and only reach out to people to shove product information and pricing down their throats, they will eventually stop picking up your calls and ignore you. If you only talk to your network when you need something and ignore them when they have something exciting or important to share, your circle of relationships will diminish.

Your prospects and your network need to know that you care so much about them and that you would do whatever it takes to maximize their success, even if it means taking a bullet for them.

For example, every day I wake up at 4:30 a.m. I write new books to help maximize my audience's potential, documenting everything that I learned to generate millions in income and $100 million in sales throughout my career. I do this because I am obsessed with helping my network learn from my failures and mistakes, and with leveraging my expertise to go from where they are today to where they want to go in the future faster and easier than they could do without gaining my knowledge.

Then I go work out and record sales podcasts and sales videos to help my network increase their sales, revenue, and income today.

Once that is done, I head into the office at Seamless.AI where we built a search engine that delivers the world's best sales leads so our audience can instantly research relevant emails and phone numbers.

Building Seamless.AI took millions of my own money, millions of investors' money, 18 hours a day 7 days a week, building the platform for years. However, I do this because I know this hard work will lead to millions of people joining the six-figure and seven-figure President's Club Awards with more than $100,000 or $1 million in sales with Seamless and our Seven Figure Sales System.

I do that exact routine seven days a week — 4:30 a.m. to 10 p.m. every single day. I take no days off to rest.

I am all-in on maximizing your success. I know people don't care how much you know until they know how much you care so I went all-in on that. I am all-in on doing whatever it takes to care for our customers, our users, our network, our employees, and anyone who follows me and our company.

I f*cking love my network. That is why I try to respond to every comment and direct message I get on social media. If you want to be successful, you have to love your network and do whatever it takes to deliver value to it. It took me my whole life to build up my network. These are the people who support me through thick or thin.

That is why everyone who reaches out and supports me with likes, comments, DMs, I get back to and engage with. I am so damn grateful to have you all in my network. It's the least I can do.

You have worked your whole life to grow your network. Make sure you don't lose it.

I treat our audience who use my products and services as a family and would do anything to help them. That is what it means to exude this habit. You need to write down what you can do in your daily routine to increase how much you care and support your network.

People don't care how much you know until they know how much you care.

BLOCK NEGATIVE PEOPLE FROM YOUR LIFE

All that was great in the past was ridiculed, condemned, and suppressed, only to emerge more triumphantly than ever before from the struggle and criticism.

Life is too short to be negative or have negative people in your life. Misery loves company and I abolished negativity and miserable people from my sales life a long time ago. If you don't, they will eventually kill you and your dreams.

Just block them.

Whether it's friends, family, or acquaintances, do what needs to be done and block them. It's like an adblocker. Once they are gone you will never look back and your dreams and goals will skyrocket.

It's like using a digital video recorder (DVR): Do you really miss every second of a commercial?!?

No!

That's what it's like blocking these types of personas from your life. These are the types of friends who really want you to fail, but say they are happy to your face.

These are the types of people who will never introduce you to anyone who might propel you forward personally or professionally.

These are the types of people who tell you that you aren't good enough…

Not smart enough…

Not rich enough…

Not skinny enough…

You name it.

Block them. Watch your accomplishments skyrocket.

One of the biggest growth hacks of my entire life was the block button on the phone and my social media. One of my favorite buttons on Linkedin is the block button!

"See ya later!" (Block.)

It's time to go all-in on going after what you know you want and deserve in this lifetime.

You've got one shot — one life — that's it.

You can do this. You got this. You deserve this.

Life is too short to be negative. Negative people are like cancer that will kill your goals and dreams. Misery loves company, so abolish negative people from your life right now.

F*CK THE HATERS AND TROLLS, BECOME BULLETPROOF

No matter what you do in life, there will be a lot of people who love you and there will be people who hate or criticize you.

For example, J.K. Rowling wrote the #1 best-selling book of all time, Harry Potter. The book has sold more than 400 million copies!!!

THE 10 BEST-SELLING BOOK SERIES OF ALL TIME

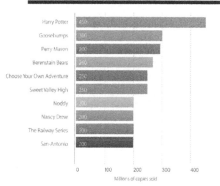

People all around the world love this book and they love the movies even more!

HARRY POTTER MOVIES WORLDWIDE GROSSES

		U.S.	WORLDWIDE TOTAL
2011	HARRY POTTER AND THE DEATHLY HALLOWS (PART 2)		$1.34 BILLION
2001	HARRY POTTER AND THE SORCERER'S STONE		$975 MILLION
2010	HARRY POTTER AND THE DEATHLY HALLOWS (PART 1)		$960
2007	HARRY POTTER AND THE ORDER OF THE PHOENIX		$940
2009	HARRY POTTER AND THE HALF-BLOOD PRINCE		$934
2005	HARRY POTTER AND THE GOBLET OF FIRE		$897
2002	HARRY POTTER AND THE CHAMBER OF SECRETS		$879

N. RAPP / FORTUNE MAGAZINE   SOURCE: BOX OFFICE MOJO

Now, I never read the book or watched the movies, but I do know it is the #1 sold book series of all time and one of the top-grossing movie series of all time.

Despite all the success that J.K. Rowling had with this book, selling hundreds of millions of copies and selling billions in movie ticket sales, there are still plenty of one-star reviews.

Take a look:

Are you kidding me? The #1 book sold of all time and the #1 box-office hit movies of all time and J.K Rowling still has haters, criticizers, and people trolling her?

This is one example of 1,000 I have saved about haters who taught me that no matter what you do in life, you will never ever please everybody.

Another extreme example is looking at the story of Jesus. Now I am not a big religious person but this guy lived his life to help others and look at how criticized he was despite being loved across the world.

No matter what I do in life, I will not and have not ever received 100 percent good reviews from my fans, followers, and audience.

So if you fall into that world of caring about haters' views, then you lose. You get caught up with sh*t that you have no control over.

People love to have an opinion. You have to understand that. People love it, they just love to have an opinion.

Every company, book, social media post, video, or product that I launch has been loved by the supporters and trashed by the critics. Everything that I have done that has gotten trashed by my critics, has gotten raving ratings and reviews by my fans and people who benefited the most from them.

They have also gone on to generate millions in sales because you make money from things you do that help positively impact others.

So, ultimately, you just have to let the talkers talk. Let the trolls troll on.

There is nothing bad about it. You should expect it because it's the new normal.

No matter what, people will love what you do and people will hate what you do.

Become bulletproof mentally, emotionally, and physically. Ignore the haters, trolls, and criticizers. Go all-in and do whatever it takes to deliver value to your customers, employees, audience, network, and fans.

AVOID PEOPLE WHO REFUSE TO ASSUME RESPONSIBILITY FOR THEIR FAILURES

When I was growing up, I used to play the blame game and blame everyone or everything as the reason I wasn't successful.

If I didn't make the varsity baseball team, it was because the coach didn't like my personality. If I didn't do well in English class, it was because my teacher was a b*tch. If I didn't get that business internship I needed, it was because the company was run by a bunch of a$sholes who didn't know what they were doing. If I was getting out of shape, it was because my family wasn't making the right healthy dinners. If my girlfriend broke up with me, it was because she was an idiot — you name it.

I would never take responsibility for anything that was bad in my life. Then something switched when I went to college. I had some type of awakening when I built my first company to $10 million in sales as a freshman, sophomore, and junior in college.

I realized that I have to assume responsibility for everything, both good and bad, in my life. If I lose a deal, it's because of me. If I can't hire that critical programmer to take the company to the next level, it's because of me. If I can't convince that girl to go out with me, it's because of me.

When you assume responsibility for your failures and successes, you gain the clarity needed to see what is holding you back from being successful.

A second example is my second company EnMobile. Since our first startup was a massive success when we launched, we thought we were the world's smartest entrepreneurs.

We didn't take any advice or listen to anyone.

Our millionaire investors told us to just build the product out of our college duplex. Instead, we got a 10,000-square-foot office space to impress my friends and family and to show the world we were the smartest entrepreneurs.

Our millionaire investors told us to spend 24/7 building and selling the product. Instead, we just focused on getting the press to tell the world about our next company. Our millionaire investors told us to bootstrap until we find the right product/market fit. Instead, we decided to burn millions of dollars and thousands of hours trying to build the product 10 different ways to sunset.

At 22, I didn't listen to anyone and I blamed everyone else for the failures I experienced.

EnMobile was the longest three-year failure of my life. One of the fastest ways to turn it around and make it successful would have been to: Listen to advice from others and assume responsibility for failure.

When you assume responsibility for everything in your life both good and bad, you see the world clearly around you and you can identify the gaps you need to fill to take you where you want to go.

Stop blaming your past, your family, your partner, or your current situation for your failures.

Your failures are because of you. No one else.

The faster you assume responsibility for your failures and everything else in your life, the faster you can change your current situation and turn your failures into massive successes.

IGNORE DOUBTERS

Doubt is a form of projection. Doubt is someone else's insecurity being pushed on you. Instead of worrying about other people's misgivings about what you are doing, create your plan. Work on your plan.

Be consistent. Be patient. Do whatever it takes. Go all out. Go big. And never let doubt hold you back from accomplishing your dreams.

Just imagine how much fun you will have when you have proven these naysayers wrong. Don't spend a lot of time delighting in their surprised faces. Double down and do the work to show them what you can do.

With all that said, the push to prove to people that you CAN fulfill your dreams is a great motivator. Dig deep into yourself and turn these doubters into believers.

Don't let them undermine your commitment to reach for the stars.

IGNORE THE PEOPLE WHO THINK THEY KNOW MORE ABOUT YOU THAN YOU DO

Typically, the people who are talking about you badly or putting you down are the ones who will never positively impact you. They will never help you go from where you're at to where you want to go to accomplish your goals.

So don't let these people give you advice. Don't take their criticisms to heart. Don't let them hold you back and don't let them stop you from achieving your potential.

What makes them think they know you best? Unless they are in your head 24/7, they cannot possibly know what you want and how hard you are willing to work to accomplish it. Don't rent out space in your head to these folks. Listen to your own heart and believe in your dreams.

If you can get great at ignoring these types of people, you will be able to truly have nothing and no one holding you back from achieving your success.

GET MOTIVATED BY THE SUCCESS OF OTHERS

Stop comparing yourself to others and using other people's success as an indicator of your failure and lack of success. When you see people who are successful, leverage their success as an opportunity for something that you too can accomplish in this life and more.

When I see someone who is more successful than me, I get ecstatic because I know that if they can accomplish that level of success, I can also accomplish that success if I put in the work and try to run with it.

Don't view other people's successes as your failure or lack of success. Like the examples above, use it as motivation and inspiration to put in the work. And realize that you can accomplish even more than what they achieved.

Continue to use other people's success as a reminder to get up and get to work.

FIND AN ACCOUNTABILITY PARTNER

As you set new massive goals and work on achieving all of your seven-figure dreams, I recommend you find an accountability partner who is there for you when the going gets tough so the tough gets going.

For me, my best friend Drew is the guy. We talk daily or weekly about our goals and dreams: how are we progressing towards accomplishing them, what is standing in our way, etc. We always hold each other accountable and call each other out when we let limiting beliefs get in the way of accomplishing our goals.

For example, I continue to challenge Drew that he needs to launch an online course and take his consulting business from 1-on-1 to 1-to-many. He's an expert in his field and can help so many people. I push him to get to his goals and he pushes me.

Every week, Drew held me accountable to finish my book series; he pushed me to get down to the body fat percentage I was striving for, and he continues to encourage me to build the dream company I have always envisioned.

Find someone who will be there for you through your successes and failures. Find someone that will be happy for you when you make it big and be there to support you when you crash and burn.

Accountability partners, coaches, and mentors are critical for achieving seven-figure success and I highly recommend them.

BET BIG ON PEOPLE IN YOUR NETWORK WHO KICK A$S

In college, I was the president of the Collegiate Entrepreneurs Organization (CEO). My partners were Jake Phillips, Blake Nolan, Michael Hopkins, Danielle Demming, and a few other great collegiate entrepreneurs. We went on to build a few different companies in college. Some did extremely well while others completely failed.

Fast forward to today, more than a decade later, when I now call these game-changers my business partners who have joined us in maximizing growth here at Seamless.AI.

When you have friends and top experts in your network who are game-changers, do whatever it takes to get them on the rocketship with you.

It's crazy how life brings you full-circle sometimes decades later. Place big bets on the best talent you know in life. It's all about making big bets on the best talent in the game—bet on the jockeys, not on the horses. The best people will do whatever it takes to overcome any challenge to become successful.

The best people will do whatever it takes. Bet big on these individuals who are game-changers in your network. The same goes for future talent and employees.

Everyone at Seamless.AI is here because I believe they will make me and everyone around them the best that they can be.

We find the best of the best and bet big on the best of the best. You need to do the same!

BUILD A NETWORK OF LIKE-MINDED HIGH ACHIEVERS

Ditch the friends who don't help you maximize your potential and replace them with friends and people in your network who motivates, inspire, educate and help you become a better person every day (personally or professionally).

You need to have a network and community of growth-minded and like-minded people where you accomplish massive achievements together. Within your network, you should be able to share all the exciting things that each of you are accomplishing and support each other through the ups and downs.

Additionally, fire all the friends who really are never happy for you when you are having success, and who are truly happy behind your back when you fail.

Since college, I built multiple seven-figure startups, I've had a lot of best friends who always supported me and I also had a lot of friends who behind my back always wished I would fail.

I fired all the friends who wanted me to fail and replaced them with true friends, mentors, and supporters who wanted to help me succeed. This worked great because I want anyone who is in my network to succeed.

You both need each other in your network to win big and learn from any challenges along the way so everyone learns together.

Skill up your network and find like-minded high achievers to replace the losers or people in your address book who aren't pushing you forward. You know what they say, "You are the average of the 5 people you spend the most time with."

Surround yourself with great people who push you forward, not backward.

Get rid of all your sh*t friends who treat you like sh*t in front of or behind your back. I promise you that you will never look back.

It's hard to cut friends out of your network but if they don't want to help you maximize your success, they aren't really true friends in the first place.

FILL YOUR LIFE WITH GREAT PARTNERS

I'm talking about your spouse, your friends, and the people who you do business with. Make sure they are all great. They need to bring great ideas, great strategies, great goals, and great challenges to you so that you can become the best that you can be.

My wife and I challenge each other every single day to maximize our potential and achieve greatness in all areas of our life. I need all of my partners in my life to try to achieve our greatest potential. If you fill your life with poor or average or mediocre partners, they will hold you back from achieving your maximum success and maximum potential.

Hang with great, be great, do great, create great, and achieve greatness. Great partners will always achieve more together then they would by themselves.

LEVEL UP YOUR FRIENDS

Level up your friends, your network, and the people who you surround yourself with. If you aim to be constantly leveling up in all facets of your life, you cannot hang out with the same groups of people you grew up with.

You want to hang out with people who have more, are doing more, who are accomplishing more, who have bigger goals, bigger dreams, bigger everything than what you have, and what you currently want. You want to hang out with the people who have been there and achieved where you want to go, in what you want to do so that you can learn how to get there.

If you keep hanging out with the same old people who are stuck in the same way of life they have always been in, you're going to become just like those people. You will become average and you will always stay stagnant with where you're at.

Instead, level up your network.

ALWAYS TRY TO GROW YOUR NETWORK AND CONNECT WITH NEW PEOPLE

Continue to connect with people who can help take you where you want to go or who you can help take where they want to go.

You just never know who in your life might need you, or might help you accomplish something now or in the future. Always work on growing your network by meeting new people, introducing yourself to others at conferences or trade shows, or on LinkedIn or on social media.

Set a goal for a number of new connections that you want to create on LinkedIn every single day. Over time, your network will grow by 5 percent, 100 percent, 1,000 percent, and upwards. My network now reaches more than 1 million people a month because every day I was focused on growing my network, and am working hard to provide them value.

Always be active in networking.

GIVE, GIVE, GIVE

The fastest way to ever get what you want in life is to help others get what they want in life. Help yourself by helping others.

You have to teach others how to become more successful and how to become even better than yourself. If you help others become as good, if not better than yourself, you always become the best that you can be.

Your success is limited if you keep the thing that generates your success a secret. Success grows from helping others achieve success. When you help others maximize their success, you increase your success and everybody increases their potential to the next level.

People support others when they believe they have a voice and are part of the decision-making authority. Work with your peers, colleagues, and customers to ensure they are contributing and a big part of the journey. Without them, you won't be successful.

ABOLISH UNPRODUCTIVE CRITICISM

If advice isn't coming from a billionaire, millionaire, or your management coaching you up, ignore it.

I've had family members criticize me for leaving a sales gig where I was making more than $1M a year to start Seamless.AI. I remember like it was yesterday, my uncle telling me it would be stupid. I remember pitching to more than 337 VCs and 297 of them all telling me we would fail because of our location, education, funding, or whatever bullsh*t criticism they threw out there.

Well, guess what? Now the company is worth over $100 million. It would've been really stupid to just keep doing what I was doing and not start this great company.

Any time you go after accomplishing your goals and dreams, there will be friends, family, co-workers, peers, and other people in your network who will criticize and judge you.

Negative criticism and judgment are normal from others.

They can't comprehend your goals and dreams. They don't even know where to start to think about trying to embark on what you are trying to accomplish.

Ignore everything that all these haters and other people are saying to try to hold you back from achieving your dreams. Instead, use it as fuel to the fire to work harder, go bigger and go all-out and all-in to accomplish your big goals.

Haters fuel my fire. I've had family, friends, best friends, co-workers, peers, industry thought leaders, competitors, and hundreds of others all hate me.

I use it as fuel, don't listen to it and just keep going forward.

If I am not being criticized, I am not going big or hard enough. I am not coming up with innovative ideas that others just comprehend or understand how to execute. Just like when I encounter fear, when I encounter criticism, I know I am thinking bigger and different than what others can truly understand.

I will never criticize you. I only want to help you accomplish whatever goals and dreams you have.

Make sure you do the same for others as well. You are either helping people get to where they want to go or you are holding them back!

DON'T COMPARE YOURSELF TO YOUR PEERS

Compare yourself to people who have 10 to 100 times what you have.

I remember when I was selling for IBM, I used to compare my results to my colleagues as I tried to beat them. The problem with this approach is that my colleagues were not achieving massive greatness. They weren't multi-millionaires or billionaires.

When I started selling for Google, instead of comparing myself to my peers, I compared myself to billionaires and set the bar insanely high. I set my own personal sales goals 3 to 5 and some even 10 times higher than my quotas.

I then figured out the daily activity to achieve these insane goals.

By comparing yourself to the legends vs. your peers, you will become limitless and achieve success in your industry, and at your company, that no one has ever achieved before.

By letting other people around you set the record, you limit your own success. You need to set the sales records, then beat them, then set them again, then beat them, then set them again, etc.

Don't compare yourself to your peers. Shoot for the stars and, if you miss, you land on the moon.

Shoot to become a billionaire and, if you miss, you join The Seven Figure Club.

Either way, this mindset will help you achieve more than you ever believed. If the mind can believe it, the mind and body can achieve it!!!

PRAISE IN PUBLIC AND SCORN IN PRIVATE

Every time someone does awesome at something, make sure you recognize it and share it with lots of people. Make them feel special and appreciated so they will replicate that success again.

Feed that personal a dose of positivity so that others around them will crave some as well. Inspire others to get your attention and to celebrate their wins.

That energy will become infectious.

On the other hand, if someone on your team messed something up, work on it with them in private. Avoid embarrassment so that you can work with them on fixing the real problem it had that caused a mistake in the first place. This creates immense respect and appreciation for you.

The person who made the error will appreciate your discretion and work harder to achieve your positive praise. When they earn it, repeat Step 1 above.

This is a great way to build an accountable team who learns from its mistakes and aims to produce better results. What a great recipe for success!

WHAT THE F*CK ARE YOU GOING TO DO FOR ME?

I wanted to get your attention because this is the only thing that anyone cares about that you are trying to sell or build relationships with.

"What's In It For Me?!" (WIIFM)

They don't care about what you want or need.

They don't care about your products and services.

They don't care about your millions raised in venture funding.

They don't care where your founders went to school. They don't care about all the awards you won.

They don't care about any of your features.

The only question they are asking themselves during every interaction with you is this one question: "What the hell are you going to do for me?"

The only way I built multiple seven-figure tech companies and sold more than $100 million in sales is because I became obsessed with answering this question and over-delivering to my prospects, customers, investors, users, followers, network, and anyone who knew me.

Don't forget to answer that question with any interaction you have with someone and you will build more profitable relationships and grow your network faster than ever before…

Every day, show your network and the people you want to do business with that you care about what you are going to do for them.

The only thing that people truly care about is for you to answer "What's in it for me?"

This applies whether you are in sales, marketing, recruiting, entrepreneurship, trying to grow your network, trying to find new friends, raising millions in new venture capital funding, working to close your first 1,000 customers, date a new partner, you name it.

Whether it's writing LinkedIn posts, launching a video series, delivering free $5,000 competitor audits, giving away complimentary strategies, texting prospects, making cold calls, working on the weekends, learning Facebook ads, launching LinkedIn ads to your named accounts, sending direct mails with value to your prospects, traveling to 10 to 100 conferences in a year, visiting prospects on-site for lunch or pitch meetings, you have to do everything that no one wants to do to maximize your sales success.

The more you do what others won't and over-deliver, the more you will learn and earn!

The more you do what others won't and over-deliver, the more you will learn and earn!

9

Take Ownership

"There is no rest for the weary. I constantly remind our employees to be afraid, to wake up every morning terrified. Not of our competition but of our customers. Our customers made our business what it is today. They're the ones with whom you have a relationship, and they're the ones to whom we owe a great obligation. We consider them to be loyal to us—right up until the second that someone else offers them a better service."
–Amazon CEO, Jeff Bezos

Ignore all the myths about your industry. Take it from me, no matter what industry or profession you're in, there will always be bullsh*t floating around about why you are working in the wrong profession. Don't fall for any of them. Ignore them, debunk them, overcome them, and set yourself free to maximize your impact on others while maximizing your income.

You are just one sales deal or life decision away from the life you want, the marriage you want, and the family you want. While I am ultimately sharing the secrets I've learned in the sales industry, the habits and beliefs shared here can be applied to any profession or position in life. Since sales skills can be used for customer service in any industry, you can learn from these regardless of what you do in your working or even professional life.

STAND FOR SOMETHING GENUINE, REAL, AND OF VALUE

Always be passionate about your work and the products you sell. You want to be so aligned with your purpose and products that everything you sell or do for customers becomes a reflection of who you are and what you stand for.

Long-term relationship building, thinking, planning, and operating are all requirements and outcomes of long-term sales success to maximize returns from your prospects and your customers. Invest your time by using the habits listed below to make the most of them.

BECOME CUSTOMER-OBSESSED
VS. COMMISSION-OBSESSED

The top salespeople are customer-obsessed. I think this is safe to say for any profession. Customer-obsessed people do whatever it takes to deliver more value to their customers and to maximize their customers' successes regardless of personal gain, personal benefits, and personal commission payouts.

Amazon CEO Jeff Bezos embodies this attitude. He proclaims, "There is no rest for the weary. I constantly remind our employees to be afraid, to wake up every morning terrified. Not of our competition but of our customers. Our customers made our business what it is today. They're the ones with whom you have a relationship, and they're the ones to whom we owe a great obligation. We consider them to be loyal to us–right up until the second that someone else offers them a better service."

Most salespeople, however, are commission-obsessed. They watch their quota and commissions, trying to do whatever it takes to beat their numbers and make more money personally. But when focusing on just the money, you're skipping the most important key to increasing your earnings.

Have a relentless drive and pursuit to develop new ways to delight your customers, whether this is new products, new technology, new pricing, or cost savings or new customer experiences. Delight your customers by transforming and enhancing the customer experience across all facets of the sales and customer lifecycle. Become obsessed with making their businesses better and they will reward you with their loyalty.

BE PURPOSEFUL

Today, more than ever before, people are working with and buying from salespeople and companies who are making a positive impact on the world.

Customers buy from people who have big purposes and missions to make the world a better place. It gives them hope for change and we all want to change for the better.

Salespeople today are not only expected to make a sale but also to step up and take ownership of societal issues and stand up for what they believe in. That's the essence of purposeful sales and empowered customers.

Find out what aligns with your customers and your company's mission, then adopt a cause or two and tie that into your brand. You will likely find that it adds to your own purpose and will promote staff morale.

BULLETPROOF YOUR SALES

People don't buy your products and services until you provide them with a bulletproof reason to buy.

People will buy from you when they are eager to:

#1) Make money
#2) Save money
#3) Save time
#4) Avoid effort
#5) Avoid / escape / remove pain
#6) Get pleasure

#7) Get recognition

#8) Increase popularity

#9) Provide for their family

#10) Protect their family

When you sell, incorporate value propositions from the list above to make your sales efforts bulletproof. You will never look back.

MAKE DEPOSITS, NOT WITHDRAWALS

I once heard this concept and it significantly impacted how I have sold and built companies from the age of 18.

Making deposits into your prospects and customers means you are giving them something of value. It's like making a deposit into your checking account or savings.

When you give something of value, it helps to take your prospects from where they are today to where they want to go tomorrow, getting closer and closer to achieving their goals and dreams. This is a deposit.

When you make a withdrawal, this means you are taking money out of your bank account. Withdrawals, as it relates to sales, means you are asking for something from the prospect. A withdrawal can be asking the prospect to book an appointment, get you an introduction or referral, or even buy your product or service.

The only way to withdraw the money and get paid by your prospects and customers is by making deposits to the point it's too damn easy for them to let you withdraw whatever you want.

For example, one of my friends wanted to work and partner with motivational speaker Tony Robbins. He knew that Tony was big into a certain type of business model, so he ended up buying a company that Tony then used to launch that business for roughly $600,000.

He approached Tony by saying, "I don't need anything. I don't want anything but I believe this will help you, so here you go."

That is a massive deposit. I bet you that deposit is going to multiply and compound over time, building an incredible relationship that maximizes the return on investment.

That is also great news about deposits. Making deposits in your prospects is like investing in the stock market or depositing money in the bank. You get to capitalize on compounding interest over time. The more deposits you make, the more compounding interest multiples that amount of money.

For those of you who don't know what compounding interest is, compounding interest means you earn money on the money you earn. For example, if you deposit $1,000 into an account with 5 percent compounding annual interest, you would earn $50 the first year. The compounding effect comes in the second year when you earn 5 percent not only on your $1,000 but also on the $50 you earned the prior year. So the second year you'd earn $52.50. In the third year, you'd earn $55.12, and each year it grows.

If you have an account where your interest compounds daily, you can earn even more.

You have to make deposits in your prospects and customers and if you eventually make enough over time, you will be able to make a withdrawal. Additionally, all of these deposits you make into the bank of your prospects create compounding interest over time so the more you make (deposits in prospects), the more you make (commissions in your bank account).

When I was selling for IBM Interactive, we put together a $50,000 strategy / creative ads campaign that we would run free of charge to Fortune 500 prospective companies we wanted to work for.

I would prospect companies like Adobe, Google, Microsoft, Dell, Oracle, and many others. When I pitched them, I'd tell them that I want to invest $50,000 worth of my team's time to put together a global ad campaign that would take that investment and generate millions in sales. The best part of all, they wouldn't pay a dime for the complimentary $50,000 strategy.

We used that deposit approach to generate tens of millions of dollars. I used it to win multi-million-dollar deals with Microsoft, Xbox, Google and YouTube, Speck Smartphone cases, Kohler, Steelcase, Sherrie-Williams, Victoria's Secret, and many others.

Another example is when I was selling for Google, we would pitch a free $10,000 paid advertising audit, strategy, and execution plan.

Then, I built Seamless.AI which crawled the web and automatically figured out the top paid search media spenders. Once I had that data, I had to prospect and sell to them.

To do that, I built a search engine to find all the digital marketers and then built an AI engine to research perfect emails and phone numbers for all these digital marketers.

Once I had the list of all the companies spending the most on paid online advertising and I had perfect contact emails and cell phone numbers for all the digital marketers, I needed an amazing DEPOSIT pitch I could make to maximize my success.

The problem was that all these top companies spending all this money on paid ads were getting pitched by hundreds of digital agencies and search marketing platforms.

That's when I decided to do a free audit, strategy, and execution plan worth $10,000. I decided to make a $10,000 deposit investment in our prospect.

In the worst-case scenario, we would learn a lot about their challenges, problems, current digital marketing landscape, goals, dreams, and where they want to go. If they don't buy from us, we can pitch others in the industry much more effectively and win new business faster.

But in the best-case scenario, they love the audit, strategy, and execution plan and pay us millions of dollars to execute the plan because we just proved that we are the experts that can take them from where they are at right now to where they want to go.

I had to pitch this concept hard to my Chief Revenue Officer at the time, but he loved the idea and approved it. We used it and, one by one by one, every pitch resulted in a 50 to 75-percent close rate.

We just kept winning and winning new clients and sold more than $100 million in Google advertising for Google, global websites, social media, and mobile programs for IBM Interactive. It was incredible.

Then we made it highly predictable, scalable, and repeatable to execute internally to deliver for new business pitches.

I wanted to share those examples of how I figured out how to make DEPOSITS (not withdrawals) with prospects in an effort to inspire and motivate you to figure out how to make deposits with your own prospects or people in your life.

Write down a list of anything and everything that you can deliver for your prospect they would love, from the most expensive solution to the cheapest. Then start to test delivering that to all of your prospects and see what sticks.

If you want to join the Seven Figure Club in sales or in life, you have to make deposits, starting today.

ALWAYS TELL THE TRUTH

Never lie, bluff, or make something up if you don't know the answer to a question.

If someone asks you something that you don't know the answer to, don't be afraid to admit that you don't know but offer to go find it for them. They will respect you and be more impressed with how you followed up with their question. Plus, it gives you a great reason to follow up.

When you don't know the answer and just make something up that is false to answer the question on the spot, you risk losing their trust and they will never forget. Don't lose your integrity and be discredited just because you don't know something or want to move fast.

No matter who it is — venture capitalists, employees, customers, or users — if I don't have the answer, I tell them I will get back to them as soon as possible with one.

LEVERAGE P (PASSION) + A (AMBITION)

People who can leverage passion and ambition will thrive in conditions of extreme uncertainty while others fail during economic depressions, economic uncertainty, and economic chaos.

The meaning of life is in the process. For me, it's my passion to maximize the sales success of every professional in the world. Every salesperson, marketer, and entrepreneur I speak with, I want to make them better and add as much value as humanly possible. If you can help someone, you get to help yourself and you constantly improve. That journey from bad to great becomes an incredible journey.

Find your passion, help people, and work hard to overcome challenges on your way to success. You will maximize your happiness, fulfillment, and success when you get to help others maximize their happiness and success.

SELL THE MAGICAL FLYING CARPET
THAT FLIES OVER THE GAP

The gap is what is missing from your prospects' vision today. You need to sell them to take them from where they are now to where they want to go. That is the gap. Sell the flying carpet that takes them to the other side.

People buy from people who are invested in maximizing their success. They don't buy from people who don't give a sh*t about them. If you do everything you can to help your prospects maximize their success, they will buy from you now or sometime in the future.

When I was younger, all I cared about was closing sales, getting commissions, and getting rich for me and my own benefit.

I wanted all the cars, big beautiful houses, amazing vacations, anything, and everything to impress as many people as possible.

The problem with only caring about yourself is that your prospects know you only give a sh*t about your commission and that you don't give a damn about them, their goals, and their needs.

People don't buy from people who don't give a sh*t about them. People buy from people who are committed to maximizing their success.

When I finally realized, at the age of like 23, that all the cars, houses, and vacations wouldn't really make me happy, and the one thing that would make me happy is helping other people become happy, that's when the riches started pouring in.

When I got rid of that "commission breath" and went all-in on doing whatever it takes to help maximize my prospects' successes, that is when I became the best that I could be and generated more pipeline and closed more sales than ever before.

An example of this is when I recognized that Seamless made me more than $1.2 million in one year. Instead of keeping this a secret weapon of mine, my team and I decided we would invest millions of dollars in helping every professional in the world use the platform. We knew that if we went all-in on helping every salesperson, marketer, and entrepreneur in the world make a lot of money that wouldn't be possible otherwise, we would make some money along the way too.

We went all-in on maximizing their success. This meant investing all of our time, capital, energy, and resources to make it happen. When prospects meet with us, they know we don't give a sh*t about any commissions. We truly want to help take them from where they are at right now to where they want to go in the future to build the life they want, the family they want, the marriage they want, and the sales commissions they want.

When the economy crashed due to the coronavirus, tens of thousands of our users on Seamless.AI didn't know how to fight through the situation and keep selling, so I started writing book after book. I realized if I shared what I learned, my prospects and users could use it to maximize their sales success and fight through the economic downturn. That's the most important thing for me right now. I want to help our users protect their families, protect their homes, and protect their incomes.

I didn't want to wake up every day at 4 a.m. to write and figure out if anyone would even want to read a book from me. I just knew the areas of sales my users were struggling with and I knew I had to document and share my expertise here to help them fight through the economic fallout arising from the pandemic.

Did I want to invest endless hours every morning and every night to write? No, but guess what? I am all-in on maximizing the success of my prospects and they know that.

People will buy from people who are invested in getting them across a gap. People don't buy from people who don't give a sh*t about them.

STOP BELIEVING YOUR QUOTA IS YOUR POTENTIAL

I always hated my quota because I always believed I could produce so much more than what was asked of me. If you think about it, your sales manager looks at the average or above-average performance of all your sales reps and decided, "Okay, this is what they should try to do based on the top 20 percent."

They will then give you that quota and ask you to beat it.

The problem with that mindset and goal setting is that it's so limited to what other people think and what other people can achieve. These people are also typically just "average." They aren't setting massive goals and dreams to one day become a seven-figure producer.

Your quota is not your potential. Like some of the habits, we already went over, when someone gives you a sales quota, multiply it by 3, 5, or 10 then reverse engineer the daily sales activity to make your new personal sales quota a reality.

The first time I made more than $100,000 a month and more than $1.2 million a year in sales was by multiplying my sales quota by five then working my a$s off every day to hit this new daily activity quota to produce 5x the quota.

It worked and it paid off big for me and I know it can for you too!

You get to define your potential and it's bigger than any quota set by any manager.

LEARN TO SELL WITHOUT SELLING

Prospects will always have their guards up when talking to salespeople. The secret to overcoming this defense is to deliver value while integrating sales objections and strategic closes right into the pitch, without your prospect even knowing.

People will put their guides up due to slimy, aggressive salespeople. If you give them value and then casually integrate sales objections and FAQs, then you can win the sale without any pressure.

Learning to sell without selling is a secret used often by the top seven-figure sales performers.

CONSISTENCY SEPARATES THE WINNERS FROM THE LOSERS

What separates the legends from the average person is really just consistency. The only time that you get great at something is if you work on becoming great at it every day, every week, every month, every year, over a long period of time.

When I started to go from making five figures in sales to six and then making six figures in sales to seven, and then to making eight figures in sales, I had goals that I was working on and accomplishing every single day, consistently. It doesn't happen overnight.

You have to break down big goals into smaller goals and work on them day in and day out, over a long period of time, to start seeing the bigger picture come together.

Consistency will separate the winners from the losers. Consistency separates people making six figures in sales from people making seven, eight, and nine figures.

Figure out what you need to do to accomplish your goals, and put consistent and persistent work effort into those activities every single day.

EARN COMPOUNDING INTEREST

It will take time for all the hard work, hard actions, hard habits, hard relationships, hard outputs, and hard effort to add up to accomplishing the big things. Therefore, you need to show up every day.

The benefits of compounding hard work and effort don't get realized until many months and years have passed, so patience is key. If you keep putting in the hard work and making the right choices that are hard to do over a long period of time, incredible returns can result.

Pure and simple compound interest reinvests your gains so they start earning a return on themselves. Those gains on your gains will pay off remarkably over time when you invest.

Just like putting deposits in the bank, the relationships and goodwill that you create with your partners will compound and grow. The trust will flourish. The willingness to pick up the phone when your company name lights up with open doors. Prospects will hear good things about your brand. Customers will be willing to increase their spending if you have impressed them with what you have invested in their time, expertise, energy, and products that work for them.

Investment king Warren Buffett often noted the power of compounded interest is unmatched by any other factor when it comes to producing wealth. Generating these gains requires patience but the longer you compound your money, the more impactful it carries.

Buffett had amassed just more than $100,000 by his mid-20s and considered himself to be essentially retired. He kept the maximum amount of his funds invested and compounding. He once joked that he viewed a long-ago $10 haircut like it was actually costing him $300,000. It turns out a $10 haircut he would have skipped in 1956 and instead invested would be worth more than $1 million today ($10 compounded at 22 percent for 58 years).

Keep in mind compounding also works in the opposite direction as well. If you have a financial advisor who charges a two-percent management fee each year, that can take a huge chunk out of your returns. Compounded over 30 years, that missing two percent cuts an investment portfolio's value in half. When it comes to compounding returns, every percentage point counts. So watch for fees or commissions that are deducted – in dollars and in goodwill.

"Those who understand compound interest earn it, and those who don't, pay it."

– Albert Einstein

TEST, OPTIMIZE, AND AUTOMATE TO MAXIMIZE SALES SUCCESS

Apply smart, strategic, and methodical sales practices.

Test new sales strategies, scripts, secrets, and ideas, searching to validate what works and then optimize the formula one element at a time. That will ensure you develop proven, strategic, specific, and long-term sales success habits.

These operating principles will generate a repeatable and consistent success formula that you and your team can stick with to maximize efforts.

Automation can also help you maximize predictable, repeatable, and scalable sales results. However, you should only automate a process once it has been tested thoroughly and proven to work repeatedly.

Then you have to figure out how you can creatively leverage technology to automate and maximize what you are doing.

This is part of the 'work smart' principle that frees up time for tasks that should no longer be manual.

TRUST DATA TO GUIDE YOUR DECISIONS

"In God we trust, all others must use data." I remember learning this famous quote by engineer Edwards Deming when I was in high school.

This habit reinforces the fact that we cannot use "hunches" or our own opinions to make the majority of our decisions.

We need to search for empirical evidence based on data to understand what is working and what is not. Then, we build on the successes of our hypothesis that we tested using data to understand the result.

In uncertain conditions or certain conditions, don't use or look for hunches. Find the facts and empirical evidence of the truth and optimize accordingly to the data.

Salespeople, sales teams, and companies have data scattered all over the place.

Become ultra-detailed, tracking, and analyzing all aspects of the sales funnel from the top to the bottom. The data will always lead you to the right decision.

CONCISELY COMMUNICATE YOUR IDEAS

Too many people can't communicate an idea quickly or concisely. In as few words as possible, always be working to improve your prospecting, pitching, and closing by sharing information concisely and quickly as possible.

If something can be said in 100 words vs. 1,000, then use 100. If something can be communicated in 10 words vs. 100, then use 10.

The world is moving to concise and quick communication. Look at the skyrocketing growth of text messaging, tweets, Instagram, Linkedin posts, etc.

Successful people, you want to work with or build profitable, successful relationships with don't have time to waste. So in all of your communication, work to be quick and concise.

SELL BY TELLING STORIES

If you want to get better at doing pretty much anything in business, learn how to tell great stories.

People will remember stories over almost anything else you say. Go through your life and document all the stories that taught you lessons that align with selling your products and services. Use them when pitching and closing prospects.

I've gone through a lot of crazy sh*t in my life so I have some wild stories from being a kid, launching seven-figure startups in college, losing millions from startups, generating $100 million in sales for IBM and Google, fundraising millions in VC capital, getting turned down by 297 VCs and building the world's fastest list building platform of all-time that helps more than 100,000 salespeople, marketers, and entrepreneurs.

I just document everything I learn on my journey and all of the stories that share my successes, failures, and everything in between.

SELL BY CONNECTING EMOTIONALLY

Remember that emotions sell. People always buy based on their emotions and then try to rationalize their purchase with logic.

The two biggest motivations for buying on emotion are always fear and desire.

Therefore try to connect with people or your prospects about their greatest fears and desires.

"When dealing with people, remember you are not dealing with creatures of logic, but creatures of emotion."

–Dale Carnegie.

People won't remember your product features, awards, company history, etc.

People will remember your stories and how you made them feel.

DRILL DOWN TO THE MOST COMPELLING PART OF THE STORY

I recommend sticking to a headline and three bullets.

Most decisions get made by groups or committees at companies and you will be relying on the people you have pitched to explain your idea to their decision-makers, bosses, peers, or colleagues. Then, they will make a decision to move forward or pass on your idea.

To be successful, you need to simplify the pitch and everything related to it so they can easily turn around and explain your idea or product to their team and get approval.

Your prospect does not need thousands of pages about features or a beautiful 10-page slide deck to sell your idea or product to their committee. They just need a headline and a few concise bullets that easily summarize the opportunity so they can easily sell it to their team for approval.

Use a headline and three bullets to communicate the most valuable parts of your proposal and capture their attention to purchase.

LIVE BY THE 60-SECOND RULE

Everything you pitch to any prospective customer must be communicated clearly, concisely, and accurately in 60 seconds or less.

You need to clearly illustrate the most valuable parts of your pitch, capture your audience's attention, and—most importantly—create the hook and urgency to inspire your prospect to take action.

Whether your call to action for your prospective customer is to learn more, book an appointment, purchase your product, etc. Create that hook and urgency to get them to take action right now and move forward with your call to action.

While many of these tips were examples given my success in sales, think about how you can apply them to any situation in your life you struggle most with. And remember, the success of any vision is determined by its **ownership** by both the leader and the people.

The success of any vision is determined by its ownership by both the leader and the people.

10

Do The Right Thing

Work and act the way that you expect others to work and act.

Leading a team is a whole new challenge for anyone who has thrived as a hard worker. It takes a different approach to get everyone firing on all cylinders to the level you expect.

The most important thing you can do is to set the right tone. Yes, you are a rock star, but your staff is not there to put you on a pedestal. You need to show them how to get the job done to your standards while empowering them so you are all working towards kicka$s goals together.

SET THE BAR TO HIGHER STANDARDS

Always work, live, and act the way you want others to operate to set the example for your team. The team will follow the attitudes, actions, and beliefs of their peers and their leaders.

Work and act the way that you expect others to work and act. Bring the team up. That means considering the tone of every message you send — in person and in writing — so it aligns with how you want people to see you and how you expect them to act.

If you get excited about a win, they will get excited about a win. If you hunker down to solve a problem without finger-pointing, they will hunker down to solve a problem without finger-pointing.

If you talk to customers in a professional and positive way, they will mirror that interaction. People will always be watching you to see how you react. Show them how you want them to act by being at your best whenever they can see you.

ALWAYS GIVE RECOGNITION TO YOUR TEAM FOR EVERY SINGLE WIN YOU ENCOUNTER

Nothing happens without an incredibly talented and hard-working team. To make everyone feel like the valuable contributor they are, make sure you recognize all of your team for their hard work, loyalty, and effort.

Regardless of if you put in 10, 25, 50, 75 or 100 percent of the work, I would rather give credit to the team and build them up then personally take credit myself just so I can feel good. Nothing happens without an incredible team.

Mix it up by delivering messages in person, sending out congratulatory emails, bringing in lunch, or treating them to a night out with a fun activity. Each type of thank-you will resonate differently with each person and you cannot express your gratitude enough to the people who help to make you succeed.

BE THE FIRST TO ASSUME RESPONSIBILITY AND TAKE THE BLAME FOR MISTAKES

If anything ever goes wrong, take the blame yourself and assume responsibility. Your team will respond with greater loyalty and admiration and will assume their own responsibility because they will respect you for accepting the ultimate responsibility for the group's performance.

You have to always assume responsibility for anything bad that happens in your life, whether in your sales career, in your business, in your marriage, your family, and all aspects of your life. Own up to it and move on.

Make sure you assume responsibility for everything bad that happens and analyze it. Figure out what you could do differently, and take steps to ensure it improves in the present and the future.

Create a culture where people can say "I messed up" so you can address and fix the problem. Then learn from it and get back to your mission.

BAN ALL FORMS OF NEGATIVITY FROM YOUR LIFE

You need to ban all forms of negativity from your personal life, your professional life, and your emotional life whether it's negative thoughts, negative limiting beliefs, negative self-doubts, negative people, negative feedback, negative ideas, negative actions, negative friends, negative family — any and all forms of negativity.

Negativity is like cancer. If you let it into your life, it will hold you back and kill all of your goals and dreams. Eventually, negativity will create a pull backward instead of propelling you light-years forward.

You don't want that type of contagion to spread within your team and affect your progress. By demonstrating a forward-looking mindset, you get the people around you to do the same.

The minute you ban all negativity from your life and only focus on positivity and surround yourself with positive ideas, positive beliefs, positive thoughts, positive people, positive habits, and everything positive, you will maximize your sales success!

ELIMINATE ALL THE THINGS
THAT STEAL YOUR TIME

You need to eliminate anything that steals your time, effort, and energy from working on the things that will get you closer to accomplishing your goals and dreams.

You know what I mean—wasting time on the news, the radio, Facebook, Instagram, worrying about what your friends are doing or what your friends are buying will not get you any closer to your dreams. In fact, it'll set you back. Eliminate all things that will set you back. Remove anything that doesn't make you feel good or lowers your self worth or personal success.

Don't think. Just cut it out. Cut out any and every behavior that doesn't help you increase your self worth and success. Smoking, drinking, gambling, over-eating, lack of working out, lack of reading, lack of working hard, you name it.

Cut out anything that doesn't challenge you to increase your success. Showing this type of discipline will inspire your team to do the same. When you're all pulling together without wasting time fiddling on your phones, you'll kick some serious a$s.

DRESS FOR SUCCESS,
EVEN IF YOU DON'T HAVE TO

You have to embody success every day and look like the person you want to become. The way you dress becomes the way you feel which becomes the way you act.

For instance, if you dress like a slob, you act like a slob, then you become a slob in all things you do.

This doesn't just mean wearing nice clothes at work. It means showing an attention to detail that people will notice. You can have the nicest suit, but if there's a stain on it and your shirt isn't pressed, you're going to send the wrong message.

Look closely in a mirror before you leave the house to make sure you have everything tucked in and you don't have a hole you didn't know about.

Even when we go out to events, we wear branded t-shirts to show we're a team. Investing in those, while wearing clean casual pants, also shows professionalism that will carry you a long way.

Dress for success and dress for the job you want, not for the job you have.

No one wants to work with a slob. Get up now, and go dress for success!

BE HUMBLE AND TREAT EVERYONE YOU MEET WITH RESPECT

From the janitor to prospective clients, investors, employees, or just new acquaintances in your life, treat everyone with respect.

For example, I raised millions in venture capital funding from a former customer of mine who then became a venture capitalist. If I didn't give that customer all the respect, hard work, and dedication to maximize his success, he would have never remembered me and never would have invested in our company.

Another example is the janitor at my office. This gentleman is so nice and always ensures that the office is spotless. I always believed in treating everyone I meet with, with the highest level of respect and appreciation.

I don't care where you come from, what your race, sexuality is, religion, or background is. After all, no one likes an as$hole! No one likes anyone who thinks they are better than everyone else.

My father drilled this into me when I was a kid because I was a talented and competitive athlete growing up. But what I remember most was whenever I got too cocky and thought I was better than my other classmates, my father would say:

"You are no better than anyone out there, you hear me? If you keep thinking you are the best, someone is going to be working harder and smarter than you, and they are going to come and beat you one day. The only way you can ensure that doesn't happen is if you work hard every day and be nice to people no matter where you come from–no matter the person, color, race, sex, background or amount of wealth."

Be humble, be nice, and try to help others.

ADD POSITIVITY TO EVERY PERSON'S DAY

Every person in this world is struggling with something. You should try to make their day just a little bit better, not worse.

Try to positively impact everyone you contact, regardless if you need something from them or not. You have no idea what they could be going through.

Ask yourself, did they leave interacting or meeting with you positively or negatively? Did you have a positive impact or negative?

If the answer is negative, you have a lot of work to change how you operate.

Treat everyone with empathy and compassion.

I treat the cleaning people who clean the office and take out our trash with the same level of appreciation that I give to our investors, employees, and everyone in our network.

You can always optimize everything you do. Having an open mind and constant hunger for improvement will help you maximize your income and maximize your results which empowers you to build long-term profitable relationships at scale.

Many people think that when they are a top performer they can degrade others or disrespect others. I don't operate this way.

My father didn't bring me up this way.

Treat everyone nicely and you will go far.

ALLOW YOURSELF TO FAIL IN PUBLIC

Risk, creativity, success, and failure are only made possible through a series of failures–some big and some small.

Hide none of them from everyone.

Take pride in your ability to recognize failure and success better than anyone else, then share your drive to learn from them to improve.

A lesson learned and not shared is a lesson lost. No one is perfect.

It's okay to go big or go home. Let others join the journey with you to cheer you on and help pick you up along the way.

I remember my father was always worried about what people thought about him. He wanted to show the perfect life to his friends, colleagues, and peers. The funny part was we were very far from the perfect family.

My father wasted so much time, money, and energy trying to show the world we had the perfect successful life, products, family, etc. that it taught me early on to just be 100 percent authentic to myself.

No one is perfect and the less perfect you are, the more relatable you are anyways.

BREAK DOWN HIERARCHIES TO ENCOURAGE OPEN DIALOGUE AND INSTIGATE COLLABORATION

This tip comes from Elon Musk's mindset on management and innovation:

"We want our leaders to find ways of motivating and inspiring their teams, reduce the noise in their work, and help remove blockers. If you are a manager or leading at any level at SpaceX, we stress that your team is not there to serve you. You are there to serve your team and help them do the best possible job for the company. This applies to me most of all. Leaders are also expected to work harder than those who report to them and always make sure that their needs are taken care of before yours, thus leading by example."

He also sent out this email to his employees at Tesla Motors:

"There are two schools of thought about how information should flow within companies. By far the most common way is a chain of command, which means that you always flow communication through your manager. The problem with this approach is that, while it serves to enhance the power of the manager, it fails to serve the company.

Instead of a problem getting solved quickly, where a person in one department talks to a person in another dept. and makes the right thing happen, other people are forced to talk to their manager who then talks to the manager in the other department who then talks to someone on his team. Then the information has to flow back the other way again. This is incredibly dumb. Any manager who allows this to happen, let alone encourages it, will soon find themselves working at another company. No kidding.

"Anyone at Tesla can and should email/talk to anyone else according to what they think is the fastest way to solve a problem for the benefit of the whole company. You can talk to your manager's manager without his permission, you can talk directly to a VP in another department, you can talk to me, you can talk to anyone without anyone else's permission. Moreover, you should consider yourself obligated to do so until the right thing happens. The point here is not random chitchat, but rather ensuring that we execute ultra-fast and well. We obviously cannot compete with the big car companies in size, so we must do so with intelligence and agility.

"One final point is that managers should work hard to ensure that they are not creating silos within the company that creates an "us vs. them" mentality or impede communication in any way. This is unfortunately a natural tendency and needs to be actively fought. How can it possibly help Tesla for departments to erect barriers between themselves or see their success as relative within the company instead of collectively? We are all in the same boat. Always view yourself as working for the good of the company and never your department."

He sets a great example of making everyone accountable without going through time-consuming webs of communicating with the "right" people. Make every person on your team the "right" person and they watch your results soar.

HIRE PEOPLE WHO MAKE YOU BETTER

Every person you bring on your team and in your network will either:

1. Make you better or 2. Make you worse.

Make sure every person you bring in your network makes you better. Remember the lessons on compound interest here as well. Really good people will spread positive energy that will spark new ideas and fire up your team to new levels.

However, really toxic people will drain that energy and turn team members against each other and the mission. Even if someone has the right skills on paper, make sure to check for attitude — positive or negative — when bringing in new blood.

Avoid #2 like the plague. They will kill your goals, dreams, and potential to achieve success.

ASK YOUR TEAM EVERY WEEK "WHAT CAN WE DO BETTER?"

The wisdom of the crowd is incredible. You hire and work with the smartest people in the world so that they can help to achieve your goals. Make sure you are tapping into the intelligence of the crowd by asking everyone every week what you can do better in sales and what you can do better for your customers.

We've generated some amazing ideas and solutions that we've executed to build one of the fastest-growing companies in the world at Seamless.AI (growing more than 500 percent year over year).

The way that we've done this is to get as many ideas from our employees, salespeople, users, customers, and investors as possible, every single day.

We have a form that lives in Google forms that allow anyone to submit an idea. They can decide if they want it to be unanimous or not. This way we get as many ideas as possible from our team on how to maximize sales performance and how to maximize customer success.

LEARN TO DELEGATE AND EMPOWER OTHERS

If you have someone who can do something better or smarter than you, delegate that task to them.

Do not try to do it just to feel accomplished or so you can control the outcome. You will only become your own bottleneck to getting things done the right way.

By trusting them to carry a task forward for you, you are telling them how much you trust them and count on them to be accountable to you and the whole team. That is one powerful hit of dopamine that they will remember.

Align tasks with people so they can grow and learn, rather than dumping work on them. Take a moment to explain why you're handing the ball to them and that you know you can rely on them.

That's the best way to build up skills and rapport while making sure the work is still going to impress the customer.

BRING OTHERS WITH YOU ON YOUR ELEVATOR RIDE UP TO THE TOP FLOOR OF SUCCESS

It takes a tribe of people to be successful. Anyone who says they have achieved mass success by themselves is lying or just plain f*cked up. You don't want to be the egotistical, cocky, non-humble, uber-successful person because when you do become successful, no one will want to hang out with you because no one likes an as$hole.

My dream has always been to become successful and to bring as many people as possible with me as we climb the ladder to success. When we get in the elevator and push the button to ride to the top floor penthouse suite, I want to have that elevator so full with others around me who I have helped that it's going to take thousands of elevators to get us all up to the party being held in the success suite.

I want my network to share in all of the successes and achievements with me. I want to win and help everyone around me win and achieve a level of success that none of us ever thought was possible because we are pushing each other up and to the next level.

Let's be real. None of my success or your success would ever be a reality without the help, love, and support from others in our network.

If you are lucky enough to do well, send the elevator back down and be sure to help out others do the same.

AUTOMATE ALL THE LOW-EFFORT AND LOW-IMPACT TASKS

Automate all the low-effort and low-impact tasks you can so you can spend all of your time, effort, energy, and money on high-impact and high-result tasks. Automate the minutia over time.

Always look for new ways to automate non-productive manual routine tasks that need to get done on a daily basis to produce the results that you need.

Also, don't feel the need to do every little thing manually if you can automate it. If there's something that you can automate, automate that specific business process in order to streamline the task so that you can focus your time and effort on those that require more strategy, creativity, and manual execution.

Think like the architect who designs a highly productive factory versus being a factory worker in that structure. One is in charge of strategy while the other does manual daily laborious manual execution. Automate and streamline the low effort and low strategic tasks and activities.

BE PREPARED AND EQUIPPED TO HAVE DIFFICULT CONVERSATIONS WITH ANYONE

Seven-figure salespeople have difficult conversations with anyone they need to, from business partners and family members to peers, spouses, friends, colleagues, and people in their network.

They deal with discussing the elephants in the room that others would prefer to ignore and avoid. They're right up-front, personal, and proactive about dealing with any issues that could snowball negatively if left unaddressed.

Tell people what they really need to hear to become better versions of themselves personally and professionally. And don't forget these difficult conversations are two-way streets. Be prepared to get candid feedback to improve as well.

Tell people what they really need to hear to become better versions of themselves personally and professionally.

11

Protect Your Dream

In order to thrive at your job, you need to function at a high level and be resilient in the face of challenges.

You cannot do this if you are tired, cranky, hungry, or distracted by details in your life that could easily be taken care of. I focus specific parts of my day to specific habits so I am in optimal shape to go out and take on the world.

Part of my approach is the mental game and some of it focuses on the physical demands on your body, plus how to handle your money. But first, let's get to the heart of the matter.

DO WHAT YOU LOVE, AND LOVE WHAT YOU DO (PART 1)

This is one of the biggest secrets I can share with you. Do what you love, and love what you do and you will never work a day in your life

I love selling amazing products that change people's lives for the better.

I literally work 14 to 18 hours a day, seven days a week all year around. Of course, I may hit a 21-day sprint and need to take a half-day or full-day off just to give the brain a break, or I may need to go on holiday with the family and take a day off, but I work seven days a week and absolutely love it every single day.

Why is that?

It's because I went all-in on doing what I love. I love sales and helping people become better so I made what I love my career– and I do it every single day.

When you get to do what you love every single day, it never feels like you are working at all.

To be honest, when I am not selling or working, I am unhappy and hate my life. I absolutely love selling. It's probably very similar to an athlete playing their favorite sport and if they were ever forced not to play, they would go nuts.

Could you imagine Lebron James being forced not to play basketball or Tom Brady not allowed to play Football? Two people I study, admire, and look up to as incredible people who have accomplished amazing things in their careers.

So when I say do what you love, I mean you really need to figure out deep down what you love and go do that all day long.

Every day I wake up ready to crush the day and work on building a sales platform to help people sell more and train them on how to generate seven figures in sales so that they can make it into our President's Club.

PART 2: LOVE WHAT YOU DO

This may come as a shock to you, but I wasn't always in love with sales.

I first loved it because I saw how my father built the first billion-dollar software company and helped provide for our family from a state of super poor to providing at a level that was very wealthy. We had everything we ever dreamed of and needed.

That's when I wanted to go into sales and start my own company.

My first company generated $10 million in sales for over three years.

I loved what I was doing, but that was right before I was about to get my a$s kicked.

When the online gambling industry crashed in the U.S., my business completely disappeared. We launched EnMobile since we believed text message marketing was the future. Unfortunately, we worked on that company for over three years, losing millions and going more than $100,000 into debt.

Long story short the company failed. I lost everything I ever owned during 2007-2009, in the height of the economic collapse.

After getting my a$s kicked and teeth knocked out, I shut down the company. I remember sitting in the office, on a late Friday night, as it was pouring rain and looking at the window.

I remember telling myself I hated entrepreneurship and sales and that I would never want to do it again. I was throwing in the towel to pursue a different career that was easier and more stable.

That following week, I kept analyzing my failure as a leader, salesperson, and entrepreneur. I read motivation and inspiration books from Napoleon Hill to Tony Robbins and many others. The theme I kept reading while I was going through this failure introspection phase was that it wasn't because of my career that failed… It was because I didn't have two things:

The technology to be successful (The lists)

The training to be successful (The sales education to prospect, pitch, and close all these B2B decision-makers)

That's when I had the massive epiphany light bulb moment.

I can't blame sales, entrepreneurship and the career I am in. I have to blame myself.

I was not assuming responsibility and doing whatever I could to get all the technologies and training I need to be successful in sales so I could:

"Do what you love and love what you do so you never work a day in your life."

You fail at your career because you aren't sold on going all-in to love what you do so you can do what you love every day.

After assuming responsibility for my failure and hate for sales and entrepreneurship, my lifestyle, mindset, and results skyrocketed.

I had all the technologies I needed to be successful and I gained all the knowledge I needed to gain to be successful at sales.

I tell this story because I didn't think I was "doing what I loved" anymore, but the reality was I didn't hate the profession of sales or entrepreneurship. The reality was I was sick and tired of working my a$s off seven days a week for three years and not making any money.

You can do anything in this world and love what you do if you learn everything you need to learn to be successful.

Stop making excuses for the things that you don't know, have, or that you can do at your job.

Sell yourself that your profession and your job is perfect for you and that you just need to get the technologies, books, and training to become the best that you can be at it.

For example, look at Michael Jordan. In college, he was cut from the Varsity basketball team. He knew he loved basketball but he started to hate it because he kept losing against his teammates...

Guess what he did?

Instead of sitting their b*tching, moaning, complaining, and quitting, he decided that for the next decade he would put in the work seven days a week and go all out to learn everything he knows about basketball and practice every day so he becomes the best that he can be.

He went on to win six NBA finals, multiple MVP Awards, ten top-scoring title records of all time, five MVP awards, ten All-NBA first-team designations, nine all-defensive first-team awards, and fourteen NBA all-star game selections. He is considered one of the greatest basketball players of all time.

What if Michael Jordan didn't put in the work to do what he loves? By investing all of his hard work, energy, and time into learning, practicing, and executing every day he eventually started winning and embodied the "Love what you do and do what you love so you never work a day in your life."

The only reason you don't love what you do and do what you love is that you aren't winning and the only reason you aren't winning is that you don't have the technologies, training, hard work, or executing the consistent, persistent, repeated actions daily to be successful.

I went from loving sales to hating sales, to loving it again because I stopped blaming my career, my upbringing, and other people for my massive failures. I finally decided to assume 100 percent responsibility and ownership for where I was at with all of my failures because I didn't have the knowledge, expertise, and technology to be successful.

Then I spent the time and money to learn everything I didn't know, I started winning again in B2B sales (almost immediately when I started at IBM Interactive) and it transformed my perceptions, mindset, and beliefs to believing again that sales and entrepreneurship was the greatest career that ever existed.

Get sold on your profession, fill the gaps, do what you love so you can love what you do… and you will never work a day in your life.

P.S. To this day I still argue with my father-in-law who thinks I work too much. He always tells me that one day I am going to be on my deathbed wishing I took off more time. This statement is complete bulls*t because I was given these amazing talents and I have cracked the code and put in the work to "love what I do and do what I love" so whenever I work, it's not working at all.

To be honest, if I stopped working on this mission to help a billion people maximize their potential and connect to opportunity, I would be lying on my deathbed looking back thinking what a wasted life I just lived.

Nothing else will really matter once you achieve this habit. It's euphoric.

INVEST IN YOUR SUCCESS

You are your greatest investment in life. Not the stock market, not real estate, not a puppy. You will pay compounding interest and dividends for a lifetime.

I've invested millions of dollars over the past decade in a half in self-improvement. I've purchased hundreds of thousands of technologies, books, Mastermind sessions, courses, coaches, mentors, and performance-improvement accountability programs.

Avoid wasting your money on expensive depreciating cars, huge houses, and exotic vacations. Instead, invest all of your money into the items I've listed above that will make you rich.

You need to sacrifice the time, energy, and capital to get everything you need today in both technology and training to take you from where you are at today to where you want to be tomorrow.

Stop worrying about what other people are buying or doing to impress your neighbors or friends. When you invest in keeping up with Joneses, you need to realize they don't really give a sh*t since they will never help you become successful.

Ultimately, the only way for you to become happy is through constant growth and improvement. By investing your money, time, energy, and capital into your future, you will maximize your chances of success and your ability to create the life, family, marriage, and sales that you always wanted to achieve!

Buy the technologies, the books, the courses, the advice, the Masterminds, the coaching, the accountability, and anything else you will need to improve.

WAKE UP EARLY AND BEAT THE COMPETITION UP

Every day, rise and grind. Every day, beat the sun up and put in the work.

Success starts early, stays up late, and never quits.

I have a saying at the office "Early bird gets the Lambo. No risk no Rari" (as in a Ferrari). We've got these posters on our wall.

Everyone has the desire, but very few have the ambition to join our Seamless Seven Figure Club.

It can be lonely waking up early, working hard, and staying late working on the road to success, but you just have to do it.

You know that if you do the work, you work hard enough, your dreams do come true.

Think about those times you get up early and you work hard; those times when you stay up late and you work hard; those times when you don't feel like working.

For example, while everyone else is sleeping in or just getting up, I want to have my workout done, my emails done and ready to hit my next appointment.

A lot of times I'm too tired, I don't want to push myself, but I do it anyway.

That is actually the dream.

It's not about the destination, it's all about the journey.

If you can understand that, what you'll see happen is, you won't accomplish your dreams, but something far bigger and greater will come out of you.

BE READY TO 'RISE AND GRIND' EVERY SINGLE DAY

When you are just getting into sales, or if you are broke and want to get into the coveted six or seven-figure club, the one thing you have actually going for you is a belief in yourself that you can actually do it.

Leverage all of your passion to accomplish this goal and go all-in relentlessly to achieve it.

You have to get up and get out on the front lines every single day working hard, taking risks, selling, networking, and making the right things happen. Then, do it over and over and over again.

Rise and grind means you have to work harder, work smarter, work more agilely and nimbly, optimize faster, do what others are doing with 10 times less money, you name it.

Be ready to outwork everyone else in your field every single day by exuding the motto "Rise and Grind."

TAKE MINI-VACATIONS AND RETIREMENTS FOUR TIMES A YEAR

I learned this habit half-way through my sales career when I was making a lot of money but was also working really long days, nights, and weekends.

I remember I was on a week-long vacation with my wife (who is a super lawyer and loves her law career as much as I love my sales career) and by days 5, 6, and 7 we were both sick of being on vacation and ready to get back to work.

We both love our work, love eating healthy, love maintaining our productive habits, and don't like getting off of our normal daily routine for too long or it takes too much work and energy to get back into those habits.

After a few days on vacation, we started getting sick of eating and drinking all day and just plain exhausted from not doing anything really productive at all.

Yes, it was amazing, fun, and relaxing to sit on the beach or layout by the pool drinking margaritas and mimosas, eating the greatest delicacies, and going sightseeing. After a while, we were sick and tired of being lazy.

When we were at lunch overlooking the ocean on an island in the Caribbean, I remember mentioning to her that I can't believe people only get to do this once a year and wait all year long to go on a nice long vacation. By the time you finally do, halfway through you are ready to get back because your body, mind, and health is urging you to get back into the system.

We started discussing and brainstorming how taking a seven-day vacation is too much for the productive human and throws off your entire routine and habits you built for work, health, and the mind. After throwing out different ideas while overlooking the beautiful crystal blue waves curling into the white sandy beaches, we had an epiphany that it would be much easier, more enjoyable, and faster to take mini-vacations / mini-retirements four times a year vs. just once a year.

We also believed saving all of your money and time to enjoy life when you are in retirement is a flawed plan. That is basically telling someone don't do much of anything enjoyable until you are in the last few years of your life.

We fundamentally disagree with this methodology and believe you can have mini-retirement vacations and enjoy life throughout the journey every year vs. only doing this the last few years of your life. So why do we recommend short vacations four times a year?

I go all-out on these 90-day sprints in sales. Many people refer to these time periods as a sales quarter. Every quarter, you have to give it your all so you crush your sales numbers, and, by the end of the 90 days, you really need a mental, physical, and emotional break to decompress and get ready for the next 90-day quarter sprint.

A sprint is an engineering and development term we use where the development team goes on two weeks sprints to get as much development done as possible. Once done, they upload it to production and start a new sprint.

For sales, every 90-day quarter is a "sprint" where you go all out and do whatever it takes to maximize the value for your prospects and close as many sales as possible.

That's when we both agreed and decided it's a no brainer to take a vacation four times a year to celebrate all the hard work accomplished in the past 90 days, rejuvenate the mind, body, and soul and prepare for the next 90-day sprint. We always take these mini-retirement vacations the first week or second week of a new 90-day sprint (quarter).

When you go on these mini-vacations or mini-retirements, I recommend not going for more than three to four days. I love going from Wednesday or Thursday evening to Sunday afternoon.

That way you only miss one or two days of work (most of the time I just work Thursday and/or Friday in the tropics anyway) and you come back midday on Sunday so you can get elevated back to reality and get back into the routine.

I love mini-retirements because it gives you something amazing to look forward to every quarter and it gives your mind, body, and soul a few days to relax and rejuvenate.

You don't want to have to look forward to vacation all year long. That is too far to sprint and still maintain excitement.

That's why my wife and I always do four mini-vacations and retirements a year. It keeps us having to work hard for something and it keeps us really looking forward to something.

Additionally, this helps you get away and enjoy life now vs. waiting until you are 65 and older enjoying life vs. enjoying your life as young as possible.

LIVE WITH NO EXTRA MONEY (NEM)

Develop a lifestyle where all of your money is being invested in the technologies, training, books, courses, and mentoring you need to maximize your returns.

This means you will have a lifestyle of no extra money. This is similar to the lifestyle of "No extra time" except all of your money goes into investing in your success–not the fancy cars, purses, houses–all the things that you buy to impress your friends and family.

Do you know what is truly impressive? Having millions in your bank account.

I live in a simple, modern townhome. I drive a simple used Mercedes.

I don't care about impressing anyone with a big house, fancy cars, etc.

I'd rather impress my friends and family with my checking account that has millions of dollars in it right now.

The only way I have seven figures in my bank account right now is because I have No Extra Money (NEM).

Every time I do, I take that money and invest it in my success.

For example, all of that money is getting reinvested back into growing my company, buying technologies to grow, courses, books, Masterminds, and coaching programs.

When you have extra money, you waste it.

When you don't have any extra money, you spend your time making it.

Take all of your money and invest in your success to become the best that you can be.

If you believe you are the greatest investment in the world, you need to go all-in on investing in your success and implementing No Extra Money (NEM).

AVOID LOSING HALF OF EVERY DOLLAR YOU MAKE

This one seven-figure habit will make you 50 percent more of every dollar you make at your job. This one habit alone will make you a million dollars and is worth just that.

Selling throughout my career for IBM Interactive and Google, I noticed I was working my a$s off to make all this money and then realized I was only earning about half of what I was making.

The government takes nearly half of everything you earn. How in the heck am I going to double my wealth and net worth if the government takes it all away?

So, I started talking with a lot of very successful millionaires, billionaires and mentors. They all recommended making sure I am maximizing the amount I am putting away into my 401k, Roth IRA, etc. Get it into any vehicle that I can invest what I earn and avoid any dilution.

I remember my Uncle Paul, who is a self-made millionaire as an accountant, coaching me by saying, "Brandon, right now you are making all this money but the way it works is for every $1 dollar you earn... you have to give 50 cents to the government. You know, in poker the casino is the house and they always take a rake at the poker tables. I replied, "Yes, I think I get it."

"Every time you get paid, it's like the government is the house and they take half of your earnings.

"But if you divert that cash instead of the dealer giving you $1 which first needs to get sliced up by the house, aka the government, you can cut out the middle man by maxing out your non-taxable earning vehicles, such as your 401ks or your Roth IRAs.

"Then, if you ever want to use that cash for investments, you can move it into a self-managed 401k where you can invest in all the stocks, mutual funds, and real estate that you want. Additionally, if it's self-managed, you can avoid a lot of the management fees that brokers take out of the pot. Essentially, you are killing two birds with one stone."

After learning this process, I immediately called my accountants and CFO and told them to max out all the non-taxable income I possibly could and put into any and all vehicles we have to put the money in.

I knew the power that compounding interest has and I knew avoiding a 50% dilution in my money didn't really add up. I truly believe losing half of what you earn just isn't fair for the hard-working Americans giving it their all today in this economy.

Ultimately, my recommendation for investments is three-fold:

Invest every dollar you have into all the technologies that you need to multiply and maximize your earning potential. By getting the technologies you need to maximize your earning potential, you will be able to put more earnings away in non-taxable vehicles. The goal is to always increase the amount of money you earn first.

After you do step 1, you need to next invest every dollar you earn into getting all the books, training, courses, and coaches needed to gain the knowledge you need to maximize your earning potential. To make seven figures in sales or to generate over seven figures net worth, you need to invest in all the education, training, and accountability to go from where you are at today to where you need to go tomorrow to be successful. This way you will learn, study, and gain the knowledge you need to fill in the gaps holding back your success.

After steps 1 and 2 are complete, work with your accountants, lawyers, CFOs, or whoever you need to so you can maximize putting away every dollar you make and avoid losing nearly half of what you earned and what is rightfully yours. There are multiple vehicles you can move your paycheck into. Start putting your money away to invest right away.

Completing steps 1 and 2 are absolutely critical because if you don't increase your income, you won't have much money to put away. That is why investing in technologies will multiply your production and earning potential.

Then getting the training will take you to the next level. Lastly, you need to take everything you earn and ensure it's getting invested with as little negative taxation hit as possible.

THE MORE MONEY YOU MAKE, THE MORE IMPACT YOU MAKE

I believe it is absolutely critical for you to maximize your income and your sales because I know the more money you make, the more impact you can make on helping others.

Do whatever it takes to make more money and invest that money into impacting more people.

I've also recognized that more money follows more impact.

The more impact you make, the more money you make. This is a revolving circular relationship. It's a never-ending continuum.

However, the minute you stop trying to achieve both is the minute you stop making more impact and making more money.

WORK OUT EVERY DAY AND EAT NOURISHING FOOD

I truly believe to maximize your professional success, you need to maximize your personal success. You can't be overweight, have a ton of diseases, be depressed or be unhealthy, and still be a top 1 percent producer. No offense to anyone that has those things. Hell, I will be the first person to tell you I have dealt with them all.

When I was first making money was when I gained the most weight because I was traveling more than 100 days a year at airports, hotels, restaurants, happy hours, events— you name it. But I hit a point where I realized I couldn't do my best work in that state. It was slowing me down.

When you get a great workout in and eat right, it sets the pace for the entire day. You can check off one of the most important yet exhausting things on your to-do list. And you also get to know that the one thing you just cranked out helped maximize your mind, body, and spirit to become the best person you can become professionally and personally.

I like working out every morning between 4:30 a.m. and 5 a.m. It allows me to get up and get to it right away. When I wake up, I don't check emails, texts, Linkedin Messages, Facebook Messages, nothing. I just get up, get dressed, and head to the gym.

I highly recommend you work out every day. Diet is also a huge part of the equation.

Eat healthily and remove anything that kills your body which, in turn, kills your productivity. If you can't control what you put in your body, how are you going to make seven figures in sales? Discipline yourself to keep your immune system thriving, so you can lead a longer, happier life celebrating your wins.

Bonus Tip: Don't make excuses about workouts or food. During the economic crash and Coronavirus Pandemic in February, March, and April of 2020, everyone had to close their gyms, restaurants, and public gatherings. Governors of states wouldn't allow you to go anywhere to prohibit the spread of the virus.

I had a complete meltdown for the first 48 hours because this destroyed my morning routine of waking up, going to the gym, crushing it for 90 minutes then getting to work.

Instead of complaining, bitching, and giving up, I remembered that I own my success. I talked to the athletic trainers in my network. I did my research on in-home workout equipment. I adapted to the changes and didn't find excuses to slack off. Find what works best for you, your body, decide to make the changes, adapt, and assume responsibility. I have to assume responsibility for everything good or bad that happens to me.

For example, deciding that I owned my success led to my decision to build an entire gym in my garage. It first started out small with dumbbells, bench, TRX, etc. Unfortunately, with COVID, all the weights were sold out across the country so I actually convinced a neighbor to sell me their weights, I found my sister-in-law had a TRX she wasn't using and then I scrambled together anything I could find to do full-body, suspension, and dumbbell workouts. I had to get inventive to continue creativing my success during COVID.

When I would go to Lifetime Fitness before the pandemic, I would burn an average of 500 calories. From that home gym, on average, I am burning 750 calories to 1000 calories per workout. So it's crazy that the home gym that I built out of necessity and the workouts I created helped me actually burn even more calories.

Moral of the story in this bonus tip: Don't make excuses for anything, assume responsibility for everything, and get to work with a workout and a nourishing meal plan for every single day of your life.

PLAN YOUR MEALS IN ADVANCE FOR THE WEEK

One way to streamline your brain processing and to maximize your health is to plan out all your meals for the week in advance. You want to batch process what you are going to eat, what you have to buy for the week etc.

This will help you eat healthily, maximize your time, and effort with thinking about what to eat and this will help you avoid making bad last-minute hungry food purchases.

Keep a record of a food journal where you write down or take pictures of the food you eat every day and identify ways that you can eat better, smarter and more healthy every day.

Eating right to maximize your health is difficult but if you want to maximize your wealth, health and potential, creating the discipline to develop healthy eating habits is critical.

By taking pictures of the food you eat every day and tracking your activity, weight etc. every day, you will have a significant amount of data and can run A/B tests on what to improve.

A/B tests are testing different days or weeks with or without trying different meals and the effects they have on your body, mind, and overall health.

DRINK 96 OUNCES OF WATER EVERY DAY

The majority of business professionals who are constantly tired is not because they need more coffee; it's because you are dehydrated and you are not drinking enough water.

On average the body of an adult human being is made up of more than 60 percent water. When these levels get lower, the body and brain get tired.

I recommend buying a 32-ounce water bottle and drinking three of them a day.

This will give your body all the water it needs to stay hydrated, maximize your success, keep your energy levels performing at maximum output and peak performance.

Before I can get a coffee, I drink water. Before I can eat, I drink water.

Build the habit to drink more water every day and shoot for 96 ounces.

WEIGH YOURSELF DAILY

I believe what gets measured gets improved. I've worked with and have been coached by a plethora of doctors, trainers, and physique bodybuilders who have all recommended tracking your weight daily, food consumption daily and activity daily.

Weighing yourself daily and writing it down in a fitness app or journal will help give you the data you need to optimize your health habits.

You can make changes with your health and match them directly to the A/B tests you are running with your food-consumption habits, activity habits, sleep habits, and water habits.

If you don't measure your weight you will never have the data or the insights to improve it.

I love journaling my weight in my Apple Activity app, Fitbit app, and Google sheet that has some custom models and algorithms to provide recommendations for optimizations when different areas improve or decrease.

INTERMITTENT FASTING

One of my best friends Drew runs a clinic called The Metabolism Wellness Clinic. He's been coaching me for the past four years and since that time I lost anywhere from 20 to 50 pounds.

The reason I was able to do this was that I became a whole-food plant-powered vegan where I lost roughly 25 pounds and then I lost another 25 pounds thanks to intermittent fasting.

Drew believes the more you can limit your food intake the more your body will burn the fat and why it's critical to push yourself to only eat between 1 and 6 p.m.

I will have a small meal at 2 p.m. every day and a moderate-sized dinner from 5 to 6 p.m every day.

I don't eat breakfast and try to avoid ever eating snacks. The media and health companies advertise you have to eat 5 to 7 times a day but the reality is humans have never had a protein deficiency ever reported in the U.S. and humans never had a slow metabolism problem ever reported in the U.S. The food industry trying to sell you to consume more food comes up with these creative angles to sell you to believe you need to eat around the clock.

The fact of the matter is the more you eat, the more weight you gain. The healthier and less you eat, the more weight you lose. Now of course it depends on the types of food you eat too (no fast food, junk food, pop, processed food, processed sugars, pop, etc).

Intermittent fasting helped me lose 25 pounds lbs and keep it off regardless of working 18 hours a day, traveling speaking around the world, and managing a company of nearly 100 employees with constant demand on going out to eat, events, travel, etc.

WEAR AN ACTIVITY TRACKING DEVICE AND SET GOALS TO BEAT EVERY DAY

I recommend getting some type of activity device to track your daily workouts, daily calories burned activity, and standing time. Personally, I think the iWatch is the most advanced on the market as well as most versatile so I recommend just going with that.

Set big daily activity goals and work to beat them every day.

By tracking your daily activity you can identify patterns and habits in your workout routine or daily life that you can optimize to maximize your health.

Also wear a sleep tracking device and work to improve your sleep every day.

Start tracking your sleep and work hard to improve your sleep habits to ensure you get a great night of deep sleep. This will help you maximize your day the following.

CREATE ROUTINES TO RELAX AND RECHARGE

To maximize your sleep, you need to create a sleep shutdown routine.

Thirty to 60 minutes before bed, I try to limit myself from working on any work that keeps my brain processing and thinking about work.

Thirty to 60 minutes before bed, I also try to prohibit any screen time such as iPhone, iPad, etc.

Thirty to 60 minutes before bed, I try to limit and prohibit any social media.

Lastly, I am working on trying to move the TV outside of the bedroom to maximize my sleep cycles but I haven't mastered this yet.

Create a routine that you follow religiously before going to bed to maximize your ability to just relax, shut down, and sleep.

Whatever is keeping you from relaxing, resting, and sleeping, try to identify and cut out of your sleep routine during those crucial 30 to 60 minutes before bed.

I shoot for completing my sleep routine 60 minutes before bed but I am also a frequent rule breaker and am working on this every day.

GO TO SLEEP EARLY

Look, this is kind of an obvious habit to implement but definitely very hard to maintain. I've never been good at going to sleep early but I am constantly working on improving every day.

I started working until midnight, then forced myself to get down to 11 p.m. and now I am finally passing out at 10:30 p.m. from waking up from 4:30 to 5 am.

I need to go to sleep early; you need to go to sleep early. We need to wake up and attack this lifetime of an opportunity in this opportunity of a lifetime right now.

We can't do that without getting enough sleep and one of the best ways to do that is by trying to get to bed earlier than when we are now.

Some tips I've gotten from mentors and friends to help go to sleep earlier is to meditate before bed, remove any lights or TVs from the bedroom, use white noise sound machines, test playing subtle meditation music, try taking melatonin, and test keeping the air conditioning cooler than hotter in the room that you sleep.

I've tried all of these things and they have helped me to sleep sooner rather than later. I hope they help you accomplish the same too!

MEDITATE DAILY

So this seven-figure habit is something that I recognized 50 to 100 CEOs do when I attended an exclusive Mastermind that cost nearly $100,000 in Beverly Hills. We stayed in a mansion and brainstormed for three days how we were going to change the world together.

The majority of the CEOs I was with were all meditating in the morning and also in the evening. It was mind-blowing.

Now I had never meditated up until that point but they educated everyone there on how meditation has consistently proven to reduce stress, lower your heart rate, improve memory, boost creativity, lower the heart rate, clear the mind and help you focus better on the most important tasks and lastly maximize emotional intelligence and wherewithal of the challenges ahead of you.

After meditating every day and night with this group, I fell in love with it. Now I do have a confession that when I got back home from the retreat I have not continued doing daily meditation. This is on my bucket list because I consistently meet with seven-figure, eight-figure, and nine-figure entrepreneurs, salespeople, and top performers who leverage meditation as a superpower to help maximize success.

I can't wait to master this habit and I hope you do too. Let me know the positive impact it makes on your life!

INVEST IN YOUR POSTURE BY GETTING A STANDING DESK AND START USING IT

The majority of your life if you are in business will be spent at a desk. It's critical that you invest in maximizing your posture so you can avoid any problems with your back, fatigue, muscle stress, tension, etc.

I invested in a sitting/standing desk and have one both at my house and at my offices. I try to stand at least 12 times a day. This is tracked on my iWatch and automatically reminds me to stand if I am not. At first, it will be very weird to work and stand and then after a while, you will really enjoy it.

You can also invest in a device you wear on your back that will vibrate if you exude poor posture. This is something I've wanted to try but haven't yet.

I want you to maximize your wealth, health, and potential. Posture is a part of living a healthy fulfilled life so think about sitting up straight more, tracking when to fix your posture, invest in a standing desk, and ensure you avoid any back or muscle problems by hunching over your desk.

I love my standing desk and think you will love it too.

12

Rise Up & Take Action

Stop making excuses. Stop waiting for tomorrow to start. Just do it now.

By now, I hope you are in the set position to do Whatever it Takes to win the race of life. As you do that, you should always keep your moral compass pointing in a direction that ensures you remain true to who you are and the place you're running toward. So far, I've touched on things like treating people well, which also says a lot about who you are. However, there are some big questions you can consider as your life goes into overdrive. It can be easy to lose your way unless you commit to your values and never stray

FIND YOUR BIGGER PURPOSE, MISSION, AND VISION THAT GOES BEYOND MONEY

If your only goal is to make a lot of money and your only mission is to buy the things that don't really matter, you will start chasing instant gratification that won't really make you happy.

When I first started my own company at 18, my only goal was to make a lot of money.

When I made more than $10 million in sales, I realized I had all the cars, the houses, and the money for vacation homes. I could do anything and everything I ever wanted to do in my entire life, yet I was the most unhappy. My only goal was just to impress everyone with the money I made.

I learned that no one cares about how much money you have. You need to stop trying to impress your family, your friends, and the people you know with the things that you buy. At the end of the day, it doesn't matter, since money alone can't sustain the ability to motivate and inspire you.

If you can stop doing things for money and start doing things because of your mission, your vision, and your purpose to change this world for the better, you will be inspired and motivated forever—period. I remember the minute I stopped chasing a commission check to benefit myself financially and changed my mission and vision to help others. Every year since that moment in time, I doubled and tripled my income! It just kept happening— boom, boom, boom—all because I was so mission-driven, knowing I had the ability to change and improve someone's life forever for the better.

No longer was it about the $25,000 commission check. Now, it was knowing that my products and services would fundamentally help others, so I had to go all out using everything I've ever learned to showcase how they can reap those benefits. By doing this, my sales, income, revenue, and personal fulfillment absolutely skyrocketed.

I started helping other people accomplish their goals, dreams, and interests. I focused on helping them get what they want in life versus selfishly worrying only about what I wanted to get out of life. **When you bring others value, they trust you, they feel loyal to you, and, in turn, the relationship is mutually beneficial**.

Once I tried to help others versus pursuing only my own financial needs, everything in my life from then on changed for the better. So, expand your vision beyond money to find the larger mission you can pursue.

FIND JOY, NOT HAPPINESS

Happiness is an emotional response to an outcome. Happiness is a shady friend who brings short-term satisfaction but never any long-term gains. It's a quid pro quo standard that you cannot sustain because you will immediately raise the bar every time you attain it.

The problem with living life seeking happiness is that it demands a certain outcome that is results reliant. If happiness is what you are living for, then you are going to be let down frequently, and you will be disappointed for most of your life.

I truly believe that chasing "happiness" is something that is temporary and then quickly disappears. One day you could be happy if you just get that house, that car, that family, that wife, but what happens after you get it?

The feeling stays there for a few hours, days, weeks, or months, and then that feeling of happiness will disappear and you will start to become unsatisfied with your life again.

The most successful people I've studied and learned from do not chase happiness. They work on growth and enjoy the ride along the way to maximizing their growth.

Enjoyment and satisfaction in the journey is much more constant and exciting to fulfill your needs than trying to generate a facade or a temporary state of happiness. For example, I am happy when I eat a big pizza or cake. That doesn't mean it's going to keep me healthy. That happiness is temporary satisfaction. That happiness is short-term gain for long-term loss. This is why working for and chasing happiness is so broken. It's a rat race that generates short-term gains for long-term losses. No one is ever happy 24/7. It's not a real thing.

If you can become completely dedicated, immersed, and satisfied when you are going through wins and losses, successes and failures, ups and downs, peaks and valleys, you will achieve ultimate euphoria with your life, personally and professionally.

For example, I hate working out every day at 4:30 or 5 a.m. It doesn't make me happy. That being said, I have fallen in love with growth and achievement and I know the short-term sacrifice to give up sleeping in to work out will maximize my health and achieve both my short-term and long-term goals. Although it's not fun, I enjoy every second because I am all-in on growth and achieving goals and dreams that I have for my life.

Another example is prospecting. Many people hate cold calling, emailing, or social selling. That being said, by putting in the work and making the calls, you will book more appointments and close more deals. It's a short-term sacrifice for short-term and long-term gains. Prospecting doesn't make you happy, however, booking new appointments and closing sales does!

It's not about "being happy," it's about doing the work and enjoying the ride to become the best that you can be.

JOY, THOUGH, IS A DIFFERENT THING

Joy is not a response to a result. It's a constant.

Joy is the feeling we have from doing what we are fashioned to do, no matter the outcome. Personally, I started enjoying my work and becoming happier when I stopped trying to make the daily labor a means to a certain end. For example, I need this company to be a multi-million success. I need my success to be acknowledged. I need the respect of my peers in sales.

All of those things are reasonable aspirations. But the truth is, as soon as the work, the daily building of the business, the doing of the deed became the reward in itself for me, I got more leads, appointments, sales, revenue, accolades, and respect than I ever had before.

You see, joy is always in process. It is a constant approach.

Focus on being alive and well in the doing of what we're fashioned to do and enjoy, remembering that time is limited. Nothing is guaranteed.

The biggest mistake that you can make in this life is to think that you have all the time in the world because you don't.

Recognizing that today is giving you the greatest opportunity of a lifetime and that tomorrow is not guaranteed will help you add gas to the fire burning inside you to get up and go all-out for your goals and dreams.

I recognized this early on in my life when I was in college and my mom got diagnosed with early Alzheimers. She lost her communication and her memory, all super early in her late 40s and early 50s. When I was 19 or 20, I got to see first hand that time is limited. Life is limited and nothing in this life is guaranteed.

My mom had a lot of goals and dreams she kept holding off on for the future but then she got Alzheimer's and all of those things were kissed goodbye.

From that point forward, I promised myself anything I want to do in this world, I would just start and learn along the way. I don't want to die a slow death, mad at myself for a life not worth living.

The biggest mistake you can make in this life is to think that you have all the time in the world because you do not.

Stop making excuses. Stop waiting for tomorrow to start. Just do it now.

RISE ABOVE WHAT OTHER PEOPLE THINK

Don't give a damn about what other people think. It will lock you up and keep you in a life of imprisonment.

Believe in yourself and what you stand for and what you could do in this world!! If you don't believe in yourself, your products, your services, or your mission in this world, nobody else will.

When I was in grade school, I would always try to act a certain way so other kids would like me, even if that wasn't truly who I was.

When I started high school, I said screw it and just was 100 percent authentic and true to my beliefs, actions, hobbies, and interests. Then, I started attracting the people who liked me, for me.

In college, I was 150 percent true to myself and my passions and interests as a salesperson and entrepreneur launching two companies that generated more than $10 million in sales. I became CEO of the Collegiate Entrepreneurs Organizations and joined the Delta Tau Delta fraternity. People loved me for me and I also cared a lot about everyone in my network wanting what was best for them whether they liked me or not.

Somehow, someway, when I got into the corporate world after my second startup EnMobile failed — when I had to go back into sales full-time — I started acting differently to fit in.

I was super buttoned-up. I would barely speak up. I would only do what I was told and would never think outside of the box. I would suck up to my boss and try to figure out whatever I can do every day to impress him.

I was so damn worried about what other people thought and I felt like I was locked in a prison of fake reality.

For anyone who knows me, I speak my mind, and I am real and 100-percent authentic to my own beliefs, never trying to fit in with others. Now, I'm finally back to being okay with others loving me or hating me because I know that no matter what, I will do whatever it takes to help you. Hopefully, that will turn some of you who hate me into fans, supporters, and followers.

Being fake and doing whatever it takes to fit in with friends, co-workers, jobs, spouses, partners, etc. will lead to a life of unfulfillment and unhappiness. Do not do it. This will eventually turn into a life of imprisonment

It is hard to not worry about what other people think and be your true self, but you just have to do it.

For example, I don't give a sh*t about sports or the news. I would rather spend seven days a week selling, building multi-million dollar companies, and working out.

This goes against everything most of my friends care about. "Hey did you catch that game?" they would say, and I would always say "No, I was working crushing it. I am playing my own game and I have to win the championship every day."

I remember a time I would waste a lot of my time watching baseball, basketball, football, and other sports to fit in instead of going after my true potential of building companies and selling millions. Of course, I love a good Ohio State football game, a Tom Brady championship comeback and, even best of all, my friend LeBron James taking my hometown Cleveland to an NBA Championship... But I won't waste a second on this stuff until the championship games or end of the playoffs, because I don't have time.

My family always used to tell me to stop working so much because one day I would be lying on my deathbed, wishing I wouldn't have worked so much. In all respectfulness, I would go tell them they are wrong.

Here is why: When you find something you need to do, something that takes over and becomes this insane passion and vision for the future, it is almost like you are drowning in an ocean, and working on it will become your next breath of air to survive. The only thing in life that you want to do is work on that passion, that vision, and that purpose. I think there are millions or billions of people who are living a life without a true mission, vision, and purpose. Those are the ones I am worried about lying on their deathbed, wishing they had figured out why they were placed here on this Earth. Those are the ones who are going to wish they went all out for what they love and believe in.

I'm going to lie on my deathbed just fine, knowing I did everything I could to go after that mission and help as many people as possible maximize their wealth, health, and potential. I am obsessed with maximizing your sales success and I think about it every second of every day. I am okay with that.

Be 100 percent the real you. Do what you are passionate about. Do what you dream. Do what you believe and go all out for your goals and dreams.

Invest purpose and passion into everything you do.

Don't care what other people think.

It will kill you and all of your goals and dreams. I won't let that happen to you.

ALWAYS STAY HUMBLE

Never believe that you are better than or more important than other people. The minute you start thinking that you are smarter, better, and faster than other people, especially those who are smarter, better, faster, and richer than you, you will fail.

Never forget everyone can teach you something that you don't know. Instead of ignoring and being dismissive of people around you, try to learn from everyone, and keep asking for their ideas, thoughts, suggestions, and feedback. If you can always be highly coachable, learning, and optimizing, you will win.

On the other hand, if you think you are better than other people at the top of the pyramid and are not willing to learn and optimize, it will hold you back from ever generating success.

BE AUTHENTIC, TRANSPARENT, AND 'IMPERFECT'

These traits will be highly valued by your customers, employees, and others in your network. Everyone has successes and failures. Everyone has good days and bad days. Everyone has things they know and things they don't. Be real about life, because everyone knows nothing is perfect.

Every single day we go through ups and downs, successes and failures, pleasure and pain, achievements and failures, wins and losses. Be authentic, real, imperfect, and be who you truly are. Full end-to-end transparency provides everyone with the 360-degree no-bullsh*t view of expectations, next steps, and results.

The days of looking like the perfect expert who never struggles are over and it's not relatable. If you want people to like you, follow you and buy from you, then you need to be real.

People trust those who communicate with the world authentically.

WRITE DOWN ONE THING YOU ARE GRATEFUL FOR EVERY DAY

This can be something good you accomplished, something positive that happened to you, whatever you want. It can be something big or something small, like being grateful to be alive.

When the going gets tough and the tough get going, when you want to quit and throw in the towel, that's when you want to start going down your list of all the amazing things you are grateful for. It will help inspire you and motivate you to keep going.

Eventually, all that sh*t will add up!

Be grateful every day. The journey is hard but good things happen every day. You just have to look closely to see that the best is yet to come.

THE MORE MONEY YOU MAKE, THE MORE IMPACT YOU CAN MAKE

I need all of you to make a lot of money because the more money you make, the more impact you can make.

In terms of leadership, the mission to serve others matters most. Employees are critical to a company's success, but we must remember why they're with you: to contribute to something bigger than you or themselves.

It's critical for you to articulate a clear purpose, mission and vision for everyone to identify with and serve. Coaching people to serve that bigger purpose every day is your job.

In management, your goal is to maximize your team's wealth, health, and potential

I run a sales tech company at Seamless.AI and believe there are 4 pillars to success for anyone's life:

- Professional life (i.e. sales job, work job, professional career)
- Family life
- Personal life (friends, personal relationships, hobbies)
- Health (diet, workout routine, healthy / not healthy)

If any one of these pillars if not a 10/10, it will negatively impact or break down the other key pillars.

My management team and I work with our team every day to ensure they are maximizing their success and becoming the best they can be professionally, personally with family and with their health.

I am all-in on maximizing the wealth, health, relationships and potential of everyone in my network.

If I am obsessed with improving the four pillars every day, I need to do the same for all of our people and anyone in my network.

I believe the #1 thing you have to care about is the success of your team and your customer.

I wholeheartedly give a sh*t about my team, because I want everyone who comes into the company, whether they stay here or go, to leave Seamless knowing it was one of the best experiences of their life.

When you truly want your team to maximize all facets of their life to be a success, you can become unstoppable.

SURROUND YOURSELF WITH PEOPLE BETTER THAN YOU

I love being surrounded by people who make me feel like I've accomplished so little or next to nothing.

Hang around people who bring you up professionally, personally, financially and health wise. If not, you will be surrounded by people who make you worse not better and they will only bring you down.

Go find mentors and rock stars who will push you to be as good as they are. They will show you, by example, what heights you can reach if you defy the odds and get everything you want out of life.

Start planning today who you can reach out to and add to your circle of friends or peers. Then get inspired by them every day. They will make you better just by being part of your life.

ASK FOR MONEY, GET ADVICE, ASK FOR ADVICE, GET MONEY TWICE

This quote from Pitbull is totally true. When I pitched 337 venture capitalists, the majority of them that I pitched looking for "money" all passed.

Then I remembered this quote and changed the pitch to ask for their advice. As the investors and venture capitalists were all giving me their advice, they all fell in love with the product and invested.

People who have succeeded in life generally love to share their expertise to help others get ahead. All you need is a short piece of their time, which is how you will pitch it to them when you ask to meet with them. Once they get to know you, it will be much easier to take that next step and bring them on as investors.

So from my perspective, he is right. "If you ask for money, you will get advice and if you ask for advice, get money twice."

NEVER DREAM ABOUT BECOMING A SUCCESS, WORK HARD TO EARN IT

Everyone wants to get everything, but virtually no one wants to work hard or sacrifice for it.

Life gives you what you deserve and what you earn. No more and no less. You are who you are and you are where you are because of you. There is no get-rich-quick scheme. There is no magic pill or magic bullet. Nothing great is ever given; it's all earned through hard work, tenacity, resiliency, positivity, grit, and by doing whatever it takes.

You have to assume responsibility for everything good AND bad in your life. Quit playing the blame game. Quit feeling sorry for yourself. Quit making bulls*t excuses as to why you can't go do something, build something, achieve something, or generate something.

You are where you are and who you are because of you. Only you can change it. Stop feeling sorry for yourself and go make sh*t happen.

For example, I grew up where my mom and dad worked four full-time jobs as lower-class Americans. I went to a babysitter who watched 30 kids and we walked through the ghetto of Cleveland to get free lunches using food stamps. Do you know how rough it is to have a kid 5 to 10 years old with 10 to 15-year-old kids going through the ghetto of the eastside of Cleveland, past homeless people, to use food stamps to grab lunch? Now, I could've looked back at that time and bitched and complained, but instead, I love that experience because it helped make me tenacious. It gave me thick skin. When I was a kid growing up and would get my a$s kicked by other older kids, it empowered me to figure out ways to stand up for myself.

Another example is when I would go to grade school and get made fun of because my mom bought all my clothes from garage sales. I should've been wearing a small T-shirt and instead was wearing really large T-shirts that were picked up at garage sales or Goodwill. I got to see all the other kids with the Michael Jordan shoes, the designer jeans, and the greatest sports gear. I went to grade school with Juan Mesa, son of Jose Mesa, one of the greatest closing pitchers of all time, and I remember sitting next to him. Juan was such a good kid, he would give me his dad's baseball stuff because he felt sorry for me.

I can use that experience and that tough upbringing as a blessing or a curse. I can use that experience as a reason for my failure or a reason for my success. I can blame everything bad that ever happened to me on my parents and my upbringing and hate them, my life, and grade school. Or I can use it as an amazing learning experience and training that taught me everything I want in life and don't want in life. Everything I need to do so I can be successful.

Going into high school, I battled some depression because of all of this but decided instead of playing the blame game to assume responsibility and start changing my life. I would apply for any jobs I could get. I worked at all the clothing stores in the mall like Abercrombie and Express because I could get 40 to 50 percent off nice clothes. I was eager to get out of my rut.

When the malls were closed or over the summer, I would work as a janitor at schools, cleaning desks because it paid a higher hourly rate. I would work at my friends' parents' companies.

I would do whatever it took to make the money I needed to change my situation.

If I can assume responsibility to change my situation at 14 and 15, you can assume responsibility for where your life is right now and decide that you are going to own all of your failures and successes, and start making the sacrifices to go out and make sh*t happen.

My father also assumed the responsibility and worked hard so by the time I was in high school, he helped change our economic situation from poor to very wealthy. He worked his a$s off with no college degree to go from a sales internship to VP of Sales building the first billion-dollar software company.

This mentality of assuming extreme ownership and extreme responsibility helped me get through all the tough times and change those tough times into great learning experiences. Believe that wherever you are today doesn't mean that has to be where you stay. You can always work hard to change where you are right now.

There are too many people who want everything but don't want to do anything for it. You are where you are at today because of you.

Instead of thinking about how difficult and hard life is, think about how great the journey has been and how incredible your story will be.

You need to accept 100 percent responsibility for everything good and bad in your life and throughout work, life, family, relationships, you name it. Even when it's not your fault, assume responsibility, and get to work fixing the problem. If you accept responsibility for everything good and bad regardless if it's because of you or not, you will have unlimited earning potential for the rest of your life.

To become successful, you will need to make sacrifices. To become successful, you will need to work hard. To become successful, you will need to be uncomfortable doing things that make you uncomfortable.

SUCCESS IS NOT BECAUSE OF LUCK

Success is not because of a magic get-rich-quick scheme. Success is not because of your background or circumstances. Nothing great is ever given and easy never pays well, I promise you. If it's easy, everyone is doing it and no one is paying someone a lot of money for something that is easy and everyone is doing.

Success is never a given. It is earned! Success will never be handed to you on a silver platter for you to eat up and run with. If you dream of being successful, there is only one way to get it and that is by putting in the work. You're never going to make the money you want or achieve the goals that you desire if you are not willing to put in the hard work, effort, and sacrifice required. It's all about developing a great strategy and executing on the strategy day in and day out, every day until your goals in your thick skull become a reality.

History forgets the losers and complainers but they always remember the winners. You know, the winners who took home that gold trophy for first place and the biggest payout for being #1 among the top 1 percent versus joining the rest of the world at the bottom 99 percent.

All great things come to those who sacrifice. The ones who sacrifice their time. The ones who sacrifice by putting in all the hard work. The ones who sacrifice their money to invest in their success with technology, training, books, you name it. The ones who sacrifice their resources today to become what they need to become tomorrow.

They do all this to achieve who they need to be to make everything they want in life, and for their family, a reality. The reason people don't succeed is that they just don't put in the work or make the required sacrifices to be successful.

You get to decide. Am I going to put in the work and make the sacrifices necessary to be successful? Or am I going to do the easy thing?

Doing the easy thing and being comfortable will leave you with an average life. That is what everyone else is doing. When you start acting, working, and thinking like everyone else, you are joining the herd of sheep. And the herd of sheep all gets slaughtered in the sea of low-income and middle-income producers.

You don't cut down a tree with one swing of the ax. It's daily, consistent, persistent, and repeated actions executed over time. You have to put in the hard work over very long-extended periods of time and when you finally assume responsibility for this and accept that is a matter of fact, you will then get over all the blood, sweat, and tears to come and just go do it. The only thing relevant to you achieving financial success and you achieving massive success are your habits, goals, hard work, and your actions. Put your head down, get to work and you will produce the results.

You will fight against the odds and become successful because you'll be willing to do whatever it takes that others won't to achieve success.

HERE IS MY GREATEST STARTUP TIP

When we started building Seamless.AI, I pitched to 337 venture capitalists. Almost all of them said no to me and my amazing team. In total, 297 of them told us we wouldn't make it.

The feedback pitching all these VCs was the same:

Your market is not good enough.
Your idea is not good enough.
Your team is not good enough.
Your education is not good enough.
Your product is not good enough.
Your development background is not good enough.
You're not good enough.

But guess what? It forced us to nail our product. It forced us to work out of my house for years. It forced us to skip doing anything that didn't improve product or sales and it forced us to always stay scrappy, nimble, cost-conscious, and humble.

It forced us to avoid doing dumb sh*t like building irrelevant features or spending capital on things that didn't maximize customer value.

The experience was hell, but we got to market fit and fast. We got to millions in sales even faster and, the best part is, we own the majority of the company.

So, I say "thank you, venture capitalists, for passing on me and our company in the past. You may have just made my team and I an extra $100 million to $500 million over the long run that we can invest in our people & customers."

There is always a silver lining.

When you think the world is coming to an end, it's always a blessing in disguise.

Keep executing, keep your head down, and believe in yourself. You will make it out on the other side.

To the investors who bet on us, I cannot wait to make you filthy rich.

Keep a ticket with your name on it for any future company we build as we continue growing 50 to 100 percent month over month.

For the 40 who bet on us, Seamless is the top-performing company in their portfolio.

See, you don't need others to believe in you.

You just need to believe that you can do it yourself.

Go get it. Go make it happen.

Don't ever let anyone ever tell you what you can or cannot do.

There will be teachers, professors, family members, and even best friends who don't believe in you.

"You aren't going to make it," they will say.

Let that be your signal to speed forward, and never look in the rear view mirror.

Use that experience as fuel in the Ferrari to never give up and make all of your goals and dreams a reality.

Don't forget, you are just one decision away from building the business you want, the relationships you want, and the life you want. It all starts by doing *Whatever it Takes* to get there.

It starts with taking big action to go make it happen today!!!!

CONCLUSION

In this book, I shared hundreds of fundamental habits, beliefs, mindsets, and secrets I have personally leveraged to build multi-million-dollar companies, generate more than $100 million in sales, and raise millions in venture capital funding.

I could have easily kept all of these lessons to myself. However, I recognize that your success is my success. I know that by doing "Whatever it Takes" to help you do the same, you will forever transform your life and become even more successful than I could ever be.

I spent more than a decade of writing, learning from, and implementing all these foundational habits into my life. I cannot emphasize enough the importance of becoming an expert at studying and applying everything you learn from this book. If you want to maximize your potential in life, you need to hone your habits, overcome limiting beliefs, and master a positive mental attitude. This book will help you do just that.

I wholeheartedly believe that if you take action today from everything you learned in this book you will maximize your revenue and generate millions—no matter who you are or where you come from.

By now, you have learned as much as possible about the qualities needed to do "Whatever it Takes." It takes just one positive change to alter your destiny forever. I promise that if you dedicate the time and put in the hard work to be successful, you will come out on the winning side, no matter the obstacles in your way.

I became a multimillionaire in sales by leveraging all the battle-tested strategies in this book, and I hope you do too. Please reach out to me with stories about your success using everything you learned in this book.

I can't wait to hear from you, reach out to me at

brandon@seamlessai.com.

ABOUT SEAMLESS.AI

Seamless.AI is the world's fastest, most accurate list building platform of all time. It's a real-time search engine powered by artificial intelligence that delivers the world's best sales leads and helps salespeople, marketers, and entrepreneurs globally automate all of their list building, prospecting, CRM data entry, and appointment setting work. This platform can be used to find emails and phone numbers for anyone in the world.

ABOUT THE SEVEN FIGURE SALES SYSTEM

As the largest power users of Seamless here at the company drinking our own champagne, having unlimited access to the Seamless.AI platform is a complete game-changer to maximize sales. We use Seamless every single day to sell and it's the number one reason we went from zero to millions in sales in record time. It's amazing to win 20-50 new customers every single day, with predictability down to the dollar and the day. However, this exciting growth also presented a massive problem for us.

Presenting Seamless at Demo Day in NJ!

Our calendars were flooded with 75-100 new qualified appointments every single day. My account executives were backed up in 5-10 demos each and every single day and we couldn't keep up with fulfilling the capacity.

When you have a sales team pitching every hour on the hour of every day, you need to be able to move fast, overcome any sales objection, and address any question that comes your way quickly.

That's when I realized it was time to triple down on writing thousands of scripts for every sales situation, objection and sales question my team and I would encounter. This way, we could quickly hear the question or sales objection and A/B test the best sales scripts to overcome and win those sales faster than ever before.

In sales, you are going to come across the same sales situations, questions, and objections every single day: "I'm Not Interested," "It's Too Expensive," "Already Working With Someone," "I Need To Talk To My Boss," "Send Me More Information," "Call Me Back Later," etc.

To build a multimillion-dollar software company, I knew that every person on my sales team needed to be fully prepared and trained for any sales situation and able to overcome any sales question or objection they would ever encounter.

As we built **Seamless.AI** from the ground up, we wrote *The Seven Figure Sales System* (a box set of over 15 books spanning thousands of sales scripts, strategies, and secrets anyone can use to generate millions in sales).

By using our Seven Figure Sales System and our Seamless.AI list building automation platform, our sales team was able to close millions in sales faster than ever before and build a multimillion-dollar business in less than a year. Within the first year, we also won Tech Company of the Year!

The team and me winning tech company of the year

Just like we decided to stop keeping Seamless.AI our secret weapon and finally share it with the world to greatly benefit, we decided to do the same with The Seven Figure Sales System and all our books, courses, and training playbooks. We needed to share it with all of you to help you accomplish the same.

Seven Figure Habits, the foundation of the *Seven Figure Sales System,* containing hundreds of pages of proven, word-for-word sales habits, beliefs, and secrets that you can use to get in the right mindset to sell any product to anyone in any market and generate millions in sales.

This book has helped us and it will help you win more sales faster than ever before.

This book is a labor of love. I know if you work hard to read it, study it, apply it, customize it, and execute selling with it, you will increase your sales, revenue, and income potential.

HISTORY & ACKNOWLEDGEMENTS

This book is a culmination of all the hard work, effort, time, capital, resources, and writing I've done throughout my 15-year sales and entrepreneurship career. This book was written in less than 30 days because these sales scripts and strategies were created, tested and saved over a decade and a half. This book would also not be possible without all the people who have positively influenced, motivated, encouraged, coached and supported me throughout my sales career. Below is a list of many of the people I would like to thank for my success. If I miss anyone on the list, trust me I am thinking of you and am forever grateful. My publishing team just told me this book is already too long as is!

Thank you all for helping me positively change the world for the better.

TO THE SEAMLESS.AI TEAM:

This book would not have been possible without our amazing team at Seamless.AI.

Most teams will tell you that you're crazy for wanting to write a book instead of focusing all of your time and energy on building a software platform like Seamless.AI. My team, however, demanded that I write these books. They knew that the strategies and secrets that helped us generate millions could help you too.

Our mission at Seamless.AI is to positively impact and empower one billion people by connecting them to opportunity faster than ever before. We believe you are one list away from the life you want. This book is directly aligned with accomplishing our mission to help you sell to that list faster than ever before.

I want to personally thank every single member on the Seamless. AI team. Thank you, Dana, Mason, Phil, Mike, Kristen, Jake, plus the sales, development, design, marketing team and support teams. All of you shape this amazing company in your own unique way and have had a massive impact on my ability to make this book a reality.

I couldn't have done it without all of you.

TO MY WIFE DANIELLE:

I first want to thank my wife Danielle and our family, The Wolf Pack. Danielle and I have been together since the launch of my first company in college and it has been one hell of a ride. We've been through many ups and downs. We've been both very rich and very poor. We go all-in always, in all ways and that takes a lot of guts and risk.

When you are an entrepreneur you sacrifice a lot to make your goals and dreams a reality. The amount of pain, suffering, and sacrifice that you have gone through to build a successful business that positively impacts one billion people, is very difficult.

Not many women could withstand, motivate, and inspire me through the endless years of ups and downs the way Danielle has every day. She is truly a superwoman and I am so grateful, humbled, and thankful to have her by my side. Danielle always believes in me, no matter how crazy my ideas get.

You have no idea how much you inspire and motivate me every day. I want to put it officially in writing how much I love you and appreciate you. I am forever grateful for everything you do to support me and help me to make the biggest impact that I can on this world.

I am so excited for what lies ahead in this incredible journey.

TO MY FATHER:

I want to thank my father David, who taught me that anything in life is possible if you can dream it, if you are willing to work your ass off and if you dedicate your life to learning how to sell. No matter the challenge that my family faced, my father always stayed positive and always found a solution no matter what. He taught me how to work hard no matter what and how to provide for my family. My father also taught me that nothing is given in this world and everything is earned. Whatever you want you need to earn it by getting up early and staying late and putting in the work. He always made me earn every penny I ever made and I am forever grateful for that.

I am where I am today because of his love, influence and his example. Dad, your sales experience has changed my life and I am going to use everything you learned and taught me to change the world and help change the lives of a lot of people for the better.

IN LOVING MEMORY OF THOSE WE HAVE LOST; YOU ARE ALWAYS ON OUR MINDS, AND FOREVER IN OUR HEARTS

TO MY MOTHER, STEPHANIE, WHOM WE LOST TO ALZHEIMER'S DISEASE:

When I was in college, my mother was diagnosed with early onset Alzheimer's disease. By the time I was 20, she couldn't even remember my name and as years passed, her memory was non-existent. Her death was devastating to my family both emotionally, financially and spiritually.

Mom, this book is an achievement and head nod to you. As I write this, I am shedding tears wishing you could have seen everything I've been able to accomplish. As a kid I would always tell you what I would accomplish one day and I know you never truly believed I would achieve any of them, not because you didn't believe in me, but instead, out of protection from how terrible of an upbringing you had. I hope no kid or human should ever have to go through what you had to endure. If your parents were alive (they are lucky they aren't), I'd get them into the ring and knock them out.

You did the best that you could do to bring us up as kids by yourself with Dad constantly travelling on the road… and for that, I am grateful. The way you raised me with tough love helped turn me into the most resilient, tenacious, whatever-it-takes, nothing-will-ever-stop-me person that I am today.

Additionally, I am so damn grateful for your Alzheimer's Disease, despite losing you to the heavens above.

You taught me life is short. Your early diagnosis inspired me to always give it my all for my goals and dreams because tomorrow isn't promised. You taught me that life is short, so just take the risk, and if you fail, who cares? Take the shot because there is nothing to lose and can all be taken away from you in an instant. This has helped me become fearless in working to accomplish my goals and everything I am striving to become as a great contributor to this world.

Losing you to Alzheimer's helped inspire Danielle and I to research all the causes of the deadliest diseases in the world. Although you may have lost your life, I think you saved my life throughout the process.

You helped me research and discover the truth about disease after college and how the food we eat can kill us or fuel us. All that research for you helped us discover that you can avoid the deadliest diseases in the world like heart disease, Alzheimer's, diabetes, cancer, etc by not eating the food that causes these diseases in the first place, like meat, dairy, processed foods, etc.

I am a whole-food, plant-powered leader because of you, and I truly believe my entire life will be lived healthier and longer than ever before. You saved my life because of all these changes I've made with my diet and I love you for that sacrifice.

Dad, Ashley and I are always thinking about you, and I hope you are resting peacefully in the heavens above.

TO MY MOTHER-IN-LAW, JANICE, IN HEAVEN

I always tell Danielle that you are an angel from above looking down on me and taking care of us all. Ever since I graduated college, your husband Don, Danielle and Kristen took me in as their own when my family was working and living out on the west coast.

Don and your kids are the greatest human beings in the world because of the amazing person you helped each of them become.

I hate cancer and I hate the pain that Danielle, Kristen and Don had to go through when you passed away. All three of them were devastated and still feel the pain until this day but I believe with loss, comes perseverance. They are working hard to change this world for the better and they couldn't have done it without you.

I also call you my angel from above for several reasons. Danielle is the best 5-star plant powered vegan chef and she always tells me she learned how to cook from you! I eat like A KING every night and wish we could have cooked and eaten together. She also helps keep our personal life and the house affairs in 5-star condition too, all of which she also says she learned from you! I don't deserve your daughter but I will work hard to keep her happy and protected every day.

You were a little entrepreneur working on so many amazing different businesses throughout your life. I know we would have had a lot of fun working on all types of crazy companies together. I am grateful you get to see all of us from above working hard to positively impact a billion others with our company today.

Your gifts bear fruits till this day. I love you and we are always thinking of you.

TO OUR INVESTORS:

I want to take the time to personally thank all of my investors for their help in making this book and our company a reality.

Today, we would not be able to support 100,000 salespeople, marketers, entrepreneurs, recruiters and companies globally if it wasn't for the group of investors that have invested in Seamless. AI, in me and in this amazing team of incredible people.

To all who invested in me and the company, we will do whatever it takes to maximize the success of your investment, the success of our customers and the success of this company.

I will do whatever it takes and always put in the work to not let you down.

SALES AUTHORS:

I want to thank all of the other sales authors out there who have impacted me beyond measure. Each of you has virtually educated, mentored and empowered me to maximize my sales success.

I am forever grateful for everything that all of you have taught me as a result of taking the time to write books of your own. I love learning from other sales experts in the industry and I'm so thankful that you took the time and energy to share your expertise and advice. I read hundreds of sales books in my early sales career and my success wouldn't be a reality without you sharing your sales wisdom with the world. I am so thankful for you.

TO THE READERS:

Thank you to all the salespeople, marketers, entrepreneurs, recruiters, and anyone else working hard to maximize your sales success. My mission in life is to positively impact a billion people and to help you connect to opportunity faster than ever before.

Without you taking the time to read this book, or investing in and using our sales software at Seamless.AI, we would never be able to accomplish this mission. This past decade I have poured my heart and soul into helping salespeople, marketers, entrepreneurs and recruiters to maximize their sales success and will continue to do so for the rest of my life.

I am forever grateful to you for buying a copy of this book, taking the time to read it, learning from it, and for writing positive reviews on it. I can't wait to hear about your success stories at **www.presidentsclubaward.com**.

This book is dedicated to all of its readers. May it help you reach your full potential and maximize your sales success every single day.

Thank you so much for believing in me and supporting my efforts.

PLEASE WRITE A REVIEW!

If this book helps you out in any way, please help me to help others by writing a review!

Everyone is searching for books to help them improve their lives for the better and the first thing they search for is the reviews.

If this book has a lot of amazing reviews with great comments, they buy the book and read it. If it doesn't have any positive reviews with great comments, they don't buy the book and read it.

I know this book can positively impact and help so many people, if we can get your support to write a great review with your comments on Amazon!

Additionally, I would love to read your review and hear how the book has helped you.

I print out every book review and hang them on my office wall to read for inspiration throughout the day. Your great review helps me personally to validate all the hard work and thousands of hours invested in writing this book for you.

Thank you again for reading this book and all of your support, I am truly honored and grateful.

I look forward to helping you make this next year your biggest and best yet!

ABOUT THE AUTHOR

Brandon Bornancin is a serial entrepreneur who built two multi-million-dollar companies and has closed over $100M in sales. Currently he is the CEO of one of the fastest SaaS companies in the US (named "LinkedIn Top 50 Startups" 2020), a motivational speaker and 18x sales author obsessed with helping sales professionals maximize their success.

As Founder and CEO of Seamless.AI, he's helped over 100,000 (and counting) companies flood their calendars and generate millions in sales using artificial intelligence to find anyone's emails and phone numbers.

Mr. Bornancin is also the author of over 15 sales books in *The Seven Figure Sales System* series containing thousands of pages of sales scripts, strategies, and secrets that he has battle-tested throughout his career to generate his success.

Mr. Bornancin is also the podcast host of "Sales Secrets From The Top 1%" and the author of *Sales Secrets From The Top 1%*, where he interviews the world's best sales experts on their top secrets to sales success.

Brandon Bornancin is also heavily involved in the community, helping spread awareness for whole-food, plant-powered living and for organizations supporting Alzheimer's disease, cancer, heart disease, diabetes, and many others. He lost his mother to Alzheimer's disease when he was in college and believes the food we consume can prevent the world's deadliest diseases.

He currently resides in Columbus, Ohio and New York, New York with his wife, Danielle Demming.

You may learn more about Brandon Bornancin at **http://www.brandonbornancin.com.**

The World's Best Sales Leads

Find Emails and Phone Numbers For Anyone.